Anonymous

Traveler's guide

Anonymous

Traveler's guide

ISBN/EAN: 9783337216696

Printed in Europe, USA, Canada, Australia, Japan

Cover: Foto ©Andreas Hilbeck / pixelio.de

More available books at **www.hansebooks.com**

NIAGARA FALLS,—FROM THE AMERICAN SHORE.

TRAVELER'S GUIDE,

AND ILLUSTRATED DESCRIPTION OF

CENTRAL NEW YORK,

NIAGARA FALLS, SARATOGA SPRINGS, ETC.

TOGETHER WITH

RAIL ROAD TIME TABLES.

BUFFALO:
FELTON & BROTHER, PUBLISHERS.
159 Main Street.
1866.

ELECTROTYPED AND PRINTED AT THE FRANKLIN PRINTING HOUSE,
BUFFALO, N. Y.

TRAVELER'S GUIDE

THROUGH

CENTRAL NEW YORK.

ALBANY.

When the peace loving Hollanders explored the Hudson in search of a suitable site for a town, or an eligible point for trading with the Indians, they selected a spot several miles above the overslaugh or shoal, with a view to security from maritime attacks by the English, then the most considerable naval power in the world. The Dutch still entertained a wholesome dread of their troublesome and arrogant neighbor, and they not unnaturally sought to shelter themselves behind a natural obstacle in the river, exposed as they must otherwise be to the rapacity of the lawless English buccaneers, who were ravaging every accessible part of the civilized world. For commercial purposes, and the transaction of general business, the situation of Albany is the worst imaginable. Seven or eight miles down the river would have avoided the shallow water which is now such a nuisance to the larger class of steamboats, and all sail craft drawing over seven feet water. And three miles further up would have avoided the precipitous acclivity which a considerable portion of the inhabitants are constrained to climb nearly every day of the year. But Mynheer values his personal security above all such considerations, and the extra labor demanded by the conditions by which he found himself surrounded, had not the weight of a feather in the scale.

Albany, the capital of the State, was described by old Jedediah Morse as a city of 1,500 houses and 7,000 inhabitants, "all with their gable ends to the street." This was sixty years ago. Now Albany contains upwards of 62,000 people. Then the quaint Dutch style of architecture, with its sharp pointed roofs and diminutive windows generally prevailed; but the Yankee spirit of innovation has crept slowly into the manners and habits of the citizens, as well as the mode in which they build their houses, and the peculiarities which formerly marked the appearance of the city have long since disappeared. The Dutch tongue was the prevailing language as late as the middle of the last century, more than a hundred years after the English had taken possession of the country, and during that period the chief improvements and additions to the city were made in the queer style of that extraordinary people. All this will appear incredible to those who look upon the array of elegant and tasteful public edifices, mansions, stores and hotels that now adorn the city.

Albany is a wealthy town, and its business men have always been distinguished for liberality, mercantile honor, and much intelligent enterprise. The consequence has been a large measure of prosperity. The society is noted for cultivation and refinement. The old Knickerbocker families, with the Patroon at their head, long constituted a class by themselves, having their own modes of recreation, and keeping people of a different lineage at arm's length. In process of time, however, the social tone became modified. More liberal views took the place of the narrow notions that had previously prevailed, and at the present time, while Albany has a well ordered and excellent society, quite different from the democratic hurly-burly of most of our western towns, there is no invidious exclusiveness, such as was formerly complained of.

Albany is a place of great business importance, both in a commercial and manufacturing point of view. The early growth of the city was exceedingly slow. At the expiration of two centuries from the period of its foundation, it numbered less than 10,000 inhabitants. Steam navigation on the Hudson, and the completion of the Erie and Champlain canals, gave it an immense impulse, and in less than half a century it gained more than 50,000 people. Standing practically at the head of navigation, and enjoying almost a monopoly of the noble Hudson, the enterprise and sagacity of its large minded merchants and capitalists, have secured for it commercial advantages such as few other cities enjoy. It is connected with New York by two lines of railway and the river, and with the great Lakes by the Central Railroad and the Erie Canal. With Canada and the North it has communication by means of the Champlain Canal and different lines of railway. Railways connect it with New England, and during the season of navigation a heavy business is transacted with different Eastern ports by way of the river and Long Island Sound. The lumber and barley markets of Albany are something wonderful. A large portion of the barley received here is converted into ale, of the best quality known to the lovers of malt. The ale is all of the choicer kinds, the modern slops, known as lager beer, being generally eschewed by the solid people of Albany.

The great workshops of the Central road, and the establishments where different articles are manufactured for that gigantic institution, give employment to more than a thousand persons. The safe, hollow ware, and iron freight car manufactory of Mr. J. M. B. Davidson, employs between three and four hundred men, turning out a million dollars worth of work a year. Seventy thousand barrels of ale are made annually at the brewery of Taylor & Son. The stoves manufactured in Albany are famous all over the country.

SCHENECTADY.

The next station is Schenectady, a cheerful old city of about 10,000 inhabitants, lying on the beautiful Mohawk, with the Erie Canal running through its centre. The distinguishing feature of Schenectady is Union College, of which **Laurens P. Hickok,** is President. This celebrated seat of science and literature, was incorporated nearly seventy years ago. The college buildings were first erected in the heart of the city, where they still remain, although in a dilapidated condition. The College now stands on an eminence in the eastern part of the town, so commanding as to overlook the whole city and the valley of the Mohawk for many miles, both east and west. The manufacturing interest of Schenectady is quite an extensive one; and it is the centre of a considerable agricultural district. The settlement of the place was commenced more than two centuries ago, and in 1690 it contained eighty houses. That year a tragic event occurred in its history. When first constructed, the city, being comparatively remote from any substantial settlement, was surrounded by palisades, with several entrance gates. Notwithstanding it was a frontier village, a quarter of a century of security had inspired general confidence among the inhabitants, and no precautions were ever taken against a nocturnal surprise. On the night of the 8th of February, 1690, some three hundred French and Indians fired the town, surprised the sleeping inhabitants, killing sixty-three and carrying off twenty-seven as prisoners. It was a bitter cold night, the ground was covered with snow, and those who escaped with their lives made for Albany, the nearest point where succor was to be obtained, many of them perishing by the way. Nearly all the buildings were burned to the ground. Three different forts were subsequently built to check the marauding bands of French and Indians. But no successful or serious attacks were afterwards made upon the town,

The growth of Schenectady has been gradual, but slow, for many years past. It is an opulent town, and contains many families distinguished for cultivation and refinement. The inhabitants are social in their habits, and dispense a liberal hospitality in admirable taste. About the middle of the last century an extensive fur trade was prosecuted from Schenectady, and this lucrative enterprise brought much treasure to the town. In 1795 it was the mart of the "Western Navigation Company," which traded with the West by means of the Mohawk, Wood Creek, and lakes Oneida and Ontario. It is now a great market for broom corn, one of the staple products of the fertile bottom lands of the Mohawk.

The railway from Troy strikes the main trunk of the Central at this point; and so does the railroad from Saratoga.

The name of the next station is HOFFMAN'S FERRY, a small hamlet in Schenectady county, about nine miles from Schenectady. John Hoffman, who formerly kept a ferry at this point, gave his name to the cluster of houses that constitute the settlement.

CRANE'S VILLAGE—is the name of the next stopping place. The first grist mill erected on the north side of the Mohawk, was built here one hundred and thirty-two years ago. For half a century the inhabitants of the German Flats, for more than fifty miles in extent, obtained their breadstuff from this mill.

AMSTERDAM—is the largest town in Montgomery county, containing upwards of four thousand inhabitants — distant about thirty-three miles from Albany. The village lies upon the left bank of the Mohawk, a pleasant situation, and exhibiting considerable architectural taste. Several manufactories are in successful operation here, the most extensive of which are an establishment for making skates, an oil factory, and a foundry and agricultural works.

About three miles from Amsterdam is JOHNSTOWN, formerly famous as the residence of the distinguished Sir William Johnson. In the early part of the last century, Admiral Warren received from George the First an extensive grant of land on which the village of Florida now stands. This was in consideration of important services rendered the English king in his wars with France. Young Johnson, a nephew of the Admiral, having just attained his majority, came out here as the agent of his uncle. The valley of the Mohawk was then an almost unbroken wilderness, where the red man hunted and fished without molestation. Johnson, who was undoubtedly a man of uncommon intellectual powers, had also great personal advantages, and his address and manners were of the most engaging description. He soon conciliated the favorable regard of the savages, and ultimately acquired an influence over them exceeding that attained by the French, including Jesuits and soldiers, during the intercourse of a century. His appointment as Indian agent, obtained through the instrumentality of his uncle, gave him additional consequence with the natives, and during his residence of nearly half a century among them, his power and authority were never diminished. He built a fine stone mansion on a small stream running through his estate, which at that time was regarded as the most imposing edifice in the colony. This he fortified as a means of defence against the French, and there he lived in true baronial style, maintaining a retinue of dependents, and dispensing a liberal hospitality.

In 1759, he led a body of two thousand Indians through the wilderness to the head of Lake George, and there defeated a large body of French under the command of a distinguished soldier. He was made a baronet and received a grant of £5,000 in money for this act of gallantry. He died in 1774, leaving his title, estate, &c., to his son John, who seems to have been greatly inferior to his father. The younger Johnson espoused the royal cause, when the revolution broke out, and he was consequently driven out of the country, his large domain having meantime been confiscated. His old mansion-house still remains in a state of good preservation. It is visible from the railway, a short distance west of Amsterdam.

Many anecdotes were formerly in circulation in the valley of the Mohawk, illustrative of the peculiarities of the Indian character, and at the same time showing the tact and adroitness of Sir William Johnson. One of them may be worth repeating here. A chief of the Mohawks who had fallen into habits of some intimacy with Sir William, became enamored of the splendid uniform of a General officer, which had just arrived from England, and after much consideration of the subject, devised a plan for obtaining possession of the gorgeous trappings. He informed Sir William that he had dreamed on the preceding night that the General had made him a present of the coat with all its decorations, and his sword besides. Sir William immediately fulfilled the Indian's dream in all its particulars. In the course of a short time the General had a dream, which he communicated to his copper colored friend. He dreamed that the Indian had given him a large and most desirable tract of land. Of course the land was granted, but the Indian protested, with many expressive gestures, that he would dream no more dreams with the General. "Ugh!" said the disconcerted savage, "you dream too big."

TRIBES' HILL—a village of about four hundred inhabitants, is situate on the Mohawk, about five miles west of Amsterdam. It stands on an eminence where the Indians were accustomed to assemble on important occasions and hold their solemn councils, hence its name. A suspension bridge spans the river at this point, which is near the mouth of Schoharie creek.

In May, 1780, Sir John Johnson made a sudden descent upon the neighborhood of his old home, in command of five hundred Indians and a band of scoundrelly tories. He attacked the settlement at Tribes' Hill, destroyed every house not occupied by a tory, and killed or captured nearly all the inhabitants. These atrocities, however, were merely incidental, the chief object of his expedition being to recover the family plate, which he had buried when driven out of the country. This he exhumed and conveyed to Canada in the knapsacks of sixty of his followers. Johnson made another predatory incursion into this region in the autumn of the same year. As before, his following was made up of tories and Indians, the latter being led by the chiefs Brandt and Cornplanter. These marauders destroyed all the property upon which they could lay their hands, and inflicted every species of cruelty upon the poor people who fell in their way. This was Johnson's last visit to the valley of the Mohawk. His tenantry were succeeded by settlers from New England, and the British Government gave him $300,000 and a command in the army, as a compensation for his losses.

INDIAN ENCAMPMENT, SHARON SPRINGS.

Take Stages at Palatine Bridge.

FONDA—about five miles from Tribes' Hill, is the capital of Montgomery county. It contains several manufactories, and a population of about seven hundred. The village was named for a Dutchman named Douw Fonda, who removed here from Schenectady, in 1751. He was murdered by the Indians under Johnson, in 1780. There is a record of the murder of two Jesuit priests at this place in 1646. These zealous and devoted men appeared in this valley on their Christian mission as early as 1640.

SPRAKER'S—is a little village of about hundred inhabitants, about nine miles west of Fonda.

PALATINE BRIDGE—a small hamlet in Montgomery county, connected with Canajoharie by a bridge across the Mohawk, is the point where passengers take the stage for Sharon Springs, a place of considerable resort during the fashionable season. The ride from Canajoharie to the Springs, a distance of some fourteen miles, is one of the most picturesque and beautiful to be found in that charming country of hill and dale. The accommodations at the Springs are ample and of the most satisfactory description. In addition to the large hotels, the Pavilion being one of the best in the country, there are several other good houses, and invalids, seeking quiet and seclusion, can find comfortable quarters in private dwellings. The mineral springs gush out from the bed of a small brook, and from a steep wooded slope on its margin. The curative properties of the waters were known to the inhabitants of the adjacent regions as long ago as the beginning of the present century, and parents often gave their distempered children the benefit of the sulphur bath; but their reputation was confined to the neighborhood until about the year 1830. Now Sharon is annually visited by fashionable people from the large cities, for purposes of relaxation and social enjoyment, quite as much as by invalids, seeking a restoration to health.

Springs furnishing water of a character totally distinct and different are often found within a few rods, and sometimes a few feet of each other. This phenomenon is seen at Van Buren, Arkansas, where the famous hot and cold springs are found. The stream from the hot spring mingles with that from the cold, not more than half a dozen rods from the fountains. The difference between the temperature of the two springs is more than 200 degrees.

A phenomenon almost as extraordinary is exhibited at Sharon. On the slope from which the streams flow, are five different springs — chalybeate, white sulphur, blue sulphur, magnesia, and pure water. The white sulphur, that is, sulphur held in solution, and the magnesia, are of the highest repute.

FORT PLAIN—three miles above Palatine Bridge, is a thriving village of about fifteen hundred inhabitants. A popular Female Academy, well conducted and well supported, contributes to the prosperity of the place. When Johnson infested the valley with his savage allies, in 1780, the men of Fort Plain were absent on military service, and the women and children took refuge in a neighboring fort for safety. When the savages prepared to invest the feeble fortification, the women, clad in their husbands' garments, stood boldly forth upon the ramparts, and so intimidated the red warriors that they retreated without attempting the reduction of the work.

Three miles from Fort Plain is a little hamlet called PALATINE CHURCH, taking its name from a stone church built here in 1770, and which is still standing. The funds for the purpose were chiefly contributed by the Nellis family, who took the wrong side in the revolution, thus saving the church from destruction when Johnson ravaged the valley. Still it was fired upon, in pure wantonness, by the marauders, and one of the bullet-holes still remains for the inspection of the curious.

ST. JOHNSVILLE—about sixty-four miles from Albany, is the next station, and quite an important one it is too; for the excellent eating-house here is extensively patronized by passengers going both ways. The village, which is named from the church of St. John, built in the township at an early period, contains about seven hundred inhabitants, and two or three considerable manufactories. Like most of the settlements on the Mohawk, St. Johnsville was a sufferer from the depredations of the Indians and their tory confederates; and for years after these wretches were finally expelled from the valley, the wrongs the inhabitants had endured still rankled in their minds, and the life of a tory who should have ventured among them would not have been worth a penny's purchase.

LITTLE FALLS.

LITTLE FALLS is a neat looking village, of nearly six thousand inhabitants, curiously built against the side of an abrupt acclivity, which rises to the height of several hundred feet, overlooking the noisy rapids in the Mohawk, from which the place takes its name. The mountain ridge, through which the river has forced its way, is a part of the chain which traverses the State from the Pennsylvania line to Lake Champlain, where it unites with the Adirondacks. The Mohawk here leaps over rocks in a turbulent cascade, making a descent of nearly fifty feet in half a mile. The gorge in the mountain is about two hundred yards in width, and through it passes the river, the canal and the Central Railroad, the cliffs on either side towering to a sufficient height to constitute a striking feature in a scene of romantic beauty. The extensive water power is made available, most of the machinery of the multitudinous manufacturing establishments, consisting of woollen and cotton factories, paper mills, flour mills, planing and saw mills, machine shops and foundries, being driven thereby. An attempt was made here to manufacture paper out of wood, and so adroitly was the first experiment made, and so plausibly were the results stated by the ingenious inventor, that a number of capitalists were induced to invest money in the enterprise. But it proved a failure. Fair paper was produced, represented to have been fabricated from basswood, but careful observation led to the conclusion that some material of longer fibre had been mixed with the wood, and the better opinion now is, that no substance of a ligneous character can be advantageously used in the manufacture.

Farming produce, in large quantities, is forwarded from this active village, especially butter and cheese. Herkimer is the largest cheese county in the State, the fertile slopes of her hills affording the finest pasture imaginable. Cheese equal to the most noted English kinds, is sent to market from the county.

In the latter part of the last century, an English gentleman—Ellice—purchased the larger portion of the village lying on the northern side of the river, and the property was held by his family until 1831. Regarding his investment as an advantageous one, Mr. Ellice declined to sell, and would only lease his lands, and the leases forbade the erection of mills or stores. The inhabitants became restiff under these onerous restrictions. They held meetings, conceived schemes for dispossessing the owners of the property; and finally managed to procure a bill to be introduced into the Legislature declaring the proprietor, as a nonresident alien, incapable of receiving rents. The question was fully discussed by able counsel, before a committee, but was finally rejected by the House of Assembly. The owners, however, were taught a wholesome lesson by the proceeding, and immediately disposed of the whole property. The purchasers sold some of the lots without the water power, and it was not until the water power became the property of a resident of the village, in 1836, that any decided improvement was effected in this great source of prosperity to the place.

HERKIMER—eight miles west of Little Falls, is the shire town of the county. The settlement was originally called "Stone Ridge," but the name was changed in honor of General Herkimer, who died from wounds received in the disastrous battle of Oriskany, in 1777. Herkimer lies on the banks of the Mohawk, and near West Canada Creek. The village was incorporated in 1807, and contains the county buildings, a paper mill and grist mill, and nearly three thousand inhabitants.

In the bloody times which followed the outbreak of the Revolution, when the Mohawk valley was the scene of many a horrible massacre, Fort Dayton, erected before the Declaration of Independence, stood near the centre of the village, and was the only refuge of the poor settlers from the cruelty of the red fiends, who hunted them as the trapper hunts the wild beast of the forest.

ILION—a place of about a thousand inhabitants, is the next station west of Herkimer. The Erie Canal also passes through it, and thus it has great advantages for the transit of goods and passengers in every direction. The principal feature of Ilion is a mammoth manufactory of arms, belonging to E. Remington & Son. More than one half of the people of the village are employed in the works. The buildings occupy an area of two acres, and present a very striking appearance. The daily manufacture of arms is not less than one hundred rifles and one hundred and fifty revolvers. A little exercise in arithmetic will satisfy one that these works alone are capable of supplying a full regiment with rifles every ten days, and a cavalry regiment with revolvers each succeeding week.

RICHFIELD SPRINGS.

Take Stages at Little Falls or Herkimer. Distance about 12 miles.

UTICA.

UTICA, a handsome, thriving and prosperous city, the second in size in all central New York, contains nearly twenty-five thousand inhabitants. It shares with Rome the honor of the county seat of Oneida, each having its court house, jail and county offices. It is one of the most important stations on the Central Railroad. Several stage routes converge to a point—the Chenango Canal connects with the Erie, the Utica & Black River Railroad, all conspiring to increase the business activity of Utica. The surrounding country is rich in agricultural productions, the butter and cheese of Oneida county being of the highest repute in the market.

The State Lunatic Asylum stands upon a fine farm on the western border of the city. The building is a spacious and costly structure, with accommodations for four hundred patients. The institution is organized and conducted with excellent judgment, every arrangement being made to suit the different kinds and degrees of insanity requiring to be treated. Gardens and shops are provided for those who are able to divert themselves by manual labor, and well chosen amusements are offered to patients whose malady is calculated to be improved by musical and theatrical diversions. The statistics of the Asylum show that a large proportion of the inmates have received essential benefit from the treatment and discipline of the institution.

The public schools of Utica are of an excellent character. The number of children attending them is about nine thousand. The district libraries contain thirty-five hundred volumes.

Visitors to Trenton Falls take the Utica & Black River Railroad cars at this point. The distance is nearly twenty miles. These Falls, now a place of great resort during the fashionable season, were scarcely known to tourists or seekers of pleasure, until 1822, when an enterprising tavern-keeper erected a house for the accommodation of visitors, near the bank of the river, between the upper and lower fall. Although neither the volume of water nor the height of the falls is of much account when compared with the majestic Niagara, or even the Genesee Falls, at Rochester, when the river is running "banks full," still the strange wildness of the surrounding scenery, united with the picturesque character of the stream, renders it a spot of extraordinary attractiveness.

ROME.

Rome is one of the largest and most prosperous villages in the State, containing a population of about ten thousand. The first settlement was made here in 1755. It was called Fort Stanwix, from a fortification constructed by General Stanwix, three or four years afterward. This fort was a formidable bastion, surrounded by a ditch and mounted with heavy cannon. A line of defences against the French, extending from Albany to Oswego, was built at an early day, and Fort Stanwix was one of the number. After the "old French war," which terminated in the surrender of Canada to the British crown, this fort fell into decay from disuse; but when the Revolution broke out, it was repaired and occupied by the Americans, under the name of Fort Schuyler. In 1777 it was invested by a considerable force, consisting of British and Indians, under General St. Ledger; but as succor approached, he raised the siege and returned to Canada.

Chittenango—a pretty village of about a thousand inhabitants, several woollen and other factories, and churches to match, thirty-seven miles from Utica, and seventeen from Syracuse. The settlement lies on the right bank of the Erie Canal, at the entrance to the narrow valley through which the Chittenango Creek, the outlet of Cazenovia Lake, makes its way to the great plain which extends from Syracuse to Rome. About a mile from the village, near the eastern bank of the stream, the famous sulphur springs of Chittenango are found. In their medicinal properties they closely resemble the celebrated White Sulphur Springs near Warrenton, Virginia. The best of testimony goes to show that they possess wonderful healing powers, especially in cutaneous affections, and diseases of the liver, stomach and bowels. In cases where the patient has a tendency to pulmonary affection, the waters, like all that contain sulphuretted hydrogen gas, seem to have an injurious effect.

The scenery in the neighborhood of the springs is picturesque and beautiful to an extraordinary degree; and at no point can the spectator enjoy it more highly than from the spacious galleries of the principal hotel. The southern view is exquisite. The fountain has been so artistically arranged, where it leaves the rocky ridge, that the waters fall in a glittering cascade, disappear, and again burst forth at the foot of a ter-

WHITE SULPHUR SPRINGS, CHITTENANGO.

race in a beautiful jet, and fill a spacious basin. Flowing from this underground, they again appear on the opposite side of the road, on the edge of the Chittenango Creek, and there present a lovely picture as they leap in mid air in several jets, and cover the rude heaps of stones around with sparkling crystals, like a hoarfrost of December. A little further south is a cottage, with rooms for recreation and refreshment. In a nook of the cliff, full fifty feet above the fountain, and reached by a winding pathway up the steep acclivity, is the gymnasium, shaded by birches and maples and some lofty oaks. In front of the house a bridge spans the rapid current of the creek; and in the noble grove across the stream are four pleasant cottages belonging to the establishment, where families reside during the season.

Here is the narrowest part of the valley; and from an eminence on the opposite side one of the most pleasing views in all that region may be obtained, including Cazenovia and Oneida lakes. The valley terminates about two miles above the springs, where the Chittenango falls perpendicularly one hundred and forty feet, and forms, in harmony with the deep gorge and other accessories, a scene of extraordinary beauty.

KIRKVILLE—a small village in Onondaga county, four miles from Chittenango, is the next station. Most of the lands in this county were assigned by the State to her soldiers at the conclusion of the war of Independence, and formed a portion of what was called the Military Tract. The land was divided into twenty-eight townships of sixty thousand acres each. This munificent benefaction amounted to one million six hundred thousand acres, of which six hundred acres were allotted to each soldier. These lands extended into eight counties, and thousands of the acres are now covered with opulent cities, towns, and villages.

MANLIUS—two miles west of Kirkville, contains several mills and factories, and a thousand inhabitants.

SYRACUSE.

Syracuse stands nearly equi-distant from Albany and Buffalo. It is an enterprising and prosperous city, containing nearly 30,000 inhabitants, and is chiefly distinguished for its very extensive salt works, and no end of salt-boilers. It is one of the most important stations on the Central road. The Syracuse & Binghamton road, and the

Syracuse & Oswego, here connect with the main trunk. Here also the old track, which runs to Rochester by the way of Auburn, Geneva and Canandaigua, strikes the main line. Scarcely a train passes over the Central from the West that does not receive a large accession of passengers at Syracuse; and the trains from the East drop about an equal number here.

The great salt springs constitute the most interesting feature of Onondaga county, of which Syracuse is the chief town. The extensive marshes bordering on Onondaga Lake are filled with brine which yields about seventeen per cent. of pure salt. In the early stage of the salt manufacture most of the wells were sunk to the depth of about thirty feet; but on making experiments, it was ascertained that the brine increased in strength as the sinkings grew deeper, and now it is drawn from a depth of 250 to 300 feet. Attempts have been made to obtain rock salt by boring upon the hills, but no traces of that mineral have ever been discovered. Different theories have been broached to account for the brine in the marshes, but its cause or source has not been satisfactorily determined. Perhaps the most ingenious notion is that which ascribes it to the constant dissolution of saline crystals supposed to reside in the shales that form a thick bed in the bowels of the surrounding hills, and which in a liquid state penetrate the marsh, where it is held by the deep and thick floor of limestone which is known to underlie the surrounding region. Considerable fanciful evidence has been adduced in support of this theory; and as no more plausible one has been started, we may as well accept it as true. Practically, the origin of the brine is of the least possible consequence. There it is in great richness and abundance, and salt now forms one of the most valuable productions of the State. During the year 1861, the enormous quantity of 7,200,371 bushels of salt were manufactured, of which 1,884,697 bushels were by solar evaporation. The State duties for that year were $72,000, and the expenses incurred by the State, in the same period, amounted to $45,000.

The first successful attempt by civilized man to extract salt from the saline waters, was made in 1789. A couple of pioneers, who had settled in Onondaga Hollow, a short distance south of the lake, having discovered the saline flavor of the waters, hung a kettle upon poles fixed in the earth, and boiling the brine for twelve hours, obtained thirteen bushels of salt. The fame of the discovery spread slowly, and five years later there were only sixty-three inhabitants in the neighborhood. And it was not until the Erie Canal was projected in 1817, that the salt boilers saw their way through the almost insurmountable difficulties of transporting such a bulky article as salt. When the canal was completed in 1825, the salt business received a great impulse. And it has gone on increasing, the increase of Syracuse proceeding in the same ratio, until the manufacture reaches nearly 30,000 bushels a day.

There is a tradition that these salt springs were known to the French before the middle of the seventeenth century; and it is known that a few French families settled in the neighborhood of Onondaga Lake, about 1660, with the acquiescence of the Indians. But the red men soon became jealous of their white neighbors, and the colonists only escaped with their lives by stealing away from their homes in the night season. A few years subsequently a second colony of Frenchmen planted themselves near the salt springs. They were all slaughtered by the Indians, under circumstances of an extraordinary nature.

The story is, that a party of Spaniards down the Mississippi, learned from the Indians that something white and sparkling, much valued by the whites, existed in limitless quantities in the country of the Onondagas. The Indians, whether ignorantly or by design, does not appear, deceived the Spaniards as to the character of the material in question. They described the mineral as a glittering substance, with which the water and the earth were both impregnated, and the Spaniards had no doubt that it was silver. They engaged an Indian to conduct them to the spot where the treasure was to be found. The Spaniards, twenty-eight in number, elate with hope, wrought their way painfully up the Mississippi to the mouth of the Ohio, ascended that stream to its source, and finally landed from the Allegany at a point near where Olean now stands. After traversing upwards of 2,000 miles of land and water, they reached the valley of the Onondagas, to find a salt deposit, instead of the expected silver. Their protracted and toilsome journey had been taken in vain; and their disappointment taking the form of rage, they quarrelled with the peaceful Frenchmen who were living quietly in the valley. The wily Onondagas fell upon the combatants, and murdered both parties, numbering about a hundred souls.

Clyde—is a place of more note, being in fact a village second only to Lyons, in the county of Wayne. It is situate on the Clyde river, the Erie canal running through its southern part. The village is in the township of Galen, so called from being a portion of the military tract assigned to the medical department of the Revolutionary army, as a recompense for its sufferings and sacrifices during the war. . At an early day the Indian traders erected a rough building there for purposes of defence, and the location was originally termed "Block House." It was used as a smuggling station by the tories, in the Revolution, and contraband goods were introduced there from Canada by way of Sodus Bay. At the time of its incorporation, the village was called Lauraville, from Laura, Countess of Bath, daughter and heiress of Sir William Pulteney; but William McNab, the agent of the great Hornby estate, changed it to Clyde, in 1818. The population is about 2,000. There is a large capital employed in various kinds of manufacturing here. Glass, of excellent quality, is made in Clyde. It has also two extensive distilleries, two steam flour mills, two steam saw mills, two furnaces and shops for the manufacture of agricultural implements, two malt-houses, a tannery, and other manufactories. The cause of religion is not neglected in Clyde, as is seen by the six temples of divine worship which adorn the village.

The bottom lands of the Clyde, and also of Mud Creek and the outlet of Canandaigua Lake, which unite and form the Clyde river, are distinguished for uncommon productiveness. They are annually overflown, and the vegetable sediment left by the flood keeps them constantly in a fine fertile condition. Tobacco, of a good quality, is raised there with signal success. Extensive fields of peppermint are noticeable on each side of the road, during the summer season. The plant is grown for making the essence, and is said to be one of the most remunerative crops that can be cultivated. About one-third of all the peppermint raised in the United States for medicinal purposes, is grown in this valley.

Wayne is rich in agricultural products, and horticulture is one of the favorite pursuits of the people. Apples, peaches and pears, are cultivated here in perfection. Wayne has derived greater benefits from the construction of the Central Railroad than almost any other county in the State. Her chief productions being of a perishable nature, transportation on the canal was too slow to be available.

LYONS.

LYONS, the capital of Wayne county, is a hundred and ninety-three miles from Albany. It stands on the Erie canal, at the confluence of Canandaigua outlet and Mud Creek, and contains about four thousand inhabitants. It is one of the prettiest villages in the State, being ornamented by a large number of handsome edifices of different descriptions. The court-house is a tasteful cut stone edifice, with a fine portico of the Ionic order of architecture, and surmounted by a towering dome. There are seven churches, some of them being of a neat style and well constructed; a union school house, where nine hundred children are taught; two banks; a great variety of stores; manufactories of different kinds, including a furnace, a machine and agricultural implement shop, pottery, brewery, fanning mill establishment, &c.

Lyons is one of the oldest towns in Western New York, a settlement having been made on the site of the village as early as 1789. Three men, with their families, numbering twelve persons in the aggregate, who had previously settled on the Mohawk, and had become discontented with their location, started west under the pilotage of an Indian trader, who was an expert navigator of the river, and finally brought up in the valley of the Clyde. The surrounding country was then an almost unbroken wilderness, and these people lived there until 1794, when permanent settlements were made on the river by Charles Williamson, the agent of the Pulteney estate. Small accessions of inhabitants were made, however, until after the close of the war of 1812, owing to the remoteness of the situation, the unfriendly feeling of the Indians, and the unsettled state of our relations with Great Britain. The general prosperity of the country which followed the peace of 1814, was only partially shared by Lyons and that portion of the State in which it is situate. And it was not until the completion of the canal, some ten years later, that the central counties of the State began to fill up at a rapid rate.

PALMYRA.

PALMYRA, twenty-three miles east of Rochester, is the last station in Wayne county. The town contains upwards of four thousand inhabitants. The population of the village is about twenty-five hundred. It contains five churches, a union school where five hundred pupils are constantly taught; a bank, and several considerable manufactories. Joseph Smith, the father of the famous Mormon prophet, who was murdered at Nauvoo, in Illinois, some fifteen years ago, settled near this village, in 1819. A short distance from the Palmyra line, on the side of a little mound, in Manchester, Ontario county, the younger Joe pretended to have discovered the plates of the famous Mormon Bible. And this was the germ of the famous system of which Brigham Young is now the apostle. The mormon Joe was a worthless vagabond and scamp from his youth up. Although married to a reputable woman, he neglected his family in the most flagrant manner, frequently absenting himself from home for long periods, and leaving them without the necessaries of life. He was strolling exhorter among the Methodists at one time, and acquired some notoriety as an extemporaneous speaker; but his tastes and proclivities were all of the most debasing description; and the unbridled license which is one of the principal features of mormon life, had its origin in the strong lusts of Joe Smith as much as in any other source. He was a scoundrel of so deep a dye that he preferred defrauding his friends and proselytes, rather than practice his rascality upon indifferent persons. He commenced his mormon schemes by ruining Martin Harris, his earliest convert to the pernicious heresy, and his whole career, until his slaughter by the outraged people of Illinois, was an unmixed series of villainies.

ROCHESTER.

ROCHESTER is a modern town, having risen from a wilderness in less than half a century. The first white child born in Rochester is still living near by, in the prime of manhood. A population of fifty thousand people now dwell about the cataracts of the Genesee, upon the spot which the early settlers of the "Genesee Country" avoided because it was swampy and unfavorable to health. Here the waters of the Genesee, in their course northward from the Allegany hills, make their last leaps ere they lose themselves in the bosom of Lake Ontario. There are four distinct cataracts within a distance of two miles, the total fall being about two hundred and fifty feet. These waterfalls affording great facilities for milling, determined the location of the town, and despite the swamps it was settled, and in a few years became as healthy and prosperous a city as there is in the Union.

Rochester was a thriving village when the great Erie canal was constructed; but that stupendous work gave a new impetus to trade here as elsewhere, and soon it became the greatest flour manufacturing town in the world. The Erie canal divides the city near its business centre, and crosses the Genesee by an aqueduct of cut stone, which cost the State more than $600,000. The Genesee Valley canal, tributary to the Erie, has its northern terminus here, its southern being at Olean, on the Allegany river.

While Rochester was making gigantic strides in her career of prosperity, and had already attained a population of more than thirty-five thousand, the great line of railway between Albany and Buffalo, since consolidated, and known as the New York Central, was completed, thus adding immensely to her facilities for trade and intercourse with the world. At this point five sections of the Central converge, viz: lines to Buffalo, to Niagara Falls, to Syracuse direct, to Syracuse by the way of Auburn, and to Charlotte at the mouth of the Genesee. The Genesee Valley R. R. extends from Rochester nineteen miles to Avon, there connecting with the Buffalo, N. Y. & Erie Railroad, giving the city railway connection with Southern New York.

Rochester has some lake trade. The Genesee is a fine harbor, and navigable waters extend within the city limits, but the business of the port is chiefly done at the mouth of the river, seven miles distant, accessible by rail.

Manufacturing in Rochester is extensive, flour taking the lead. From 600,000 to 1.000,000 bbls. of flour are made here annually. Other branches of manufacturing are prosperous. The mercantile business is considerable, as a population of nearly half a million people are within two hours travel by rail of the city.

Rochester has been not inaptly styled a city of foliage and flowers. Ornamental trees are cultivated with care, and the growth of fruit trees in the town and adjacent country is extensive. Here are the great nurseries of the American continent. Thousands of acres within five miles of the centre of Rochester are devoted to the culture of fruit trees and ornamental shrubs, and millions of trees are annually sent abroad to distant counties, States, and even to foreign countries. The annual product of these nurseries is valued at $2,000,000.

Situated in the centre of the most fertile region of New York State, surrounded with a population of industrious and wealthy farmers, it is not strange that Rochester is a flourishing city. The wealth that her citizens have accumulated has not been hoarded, but has been lavishly bestowed, so as to add to the beauty of the town and enhance the comfort of the people. There are nearly thirty miles of improved streets — including many finely paved with stone. There are twenty-five miles of excellent sewerage; nearly one thousand street gas lamps, a dozen spacious parks, four elegant bridges over the Genesee — including one of cut stone, costing nearly $100,000, upon which are fine blocks of brick stores; and there are many handsome public buildings: the court house and city hall cost $80,000. There are eighteen public school houses, some of which cost $15,000 each; fifty churches, the best of which cost $70,000. The University of Rochester, a popular college, is situated in the eastern part of the city, near the Central railroad. The Western House of Refuge, a State reform school for boys, is situated in the northern part of the city, and the immense pile of buildings can be seen from the Rochester & Niagara Falls Railroad. There are two large hospitals — one under the management of the Sisters of Charity, the other a city institution.

A line of street railways, seventeen miles in length, is being constructed by a company, who will complete ten miles by the summer of 1863.

Mt. Hope Cemetery, in the south part of Rochester, two miles from the Central Railroad, is an object of local pride, and is visited annually by thousands of strangers. The cemetery contains about one hundred acres of hill and dale, thickly studded with forest trees, and beautified by the expenditure of many thousands in making its winding paths, towering monuments, massive tombs and grassy mounds, pleasing to the eye and becoming to the "City of the Dead." Mt. Hope has not received that lavish expenditure of wealth bestowed upon Mt. Auburn or Greenwood, but in natural advantages it vastly excels both.

The traveler who crosses Rochester by the Central Railroad, has but a faint idea of the town, for he sees but little of it, and that by no means the most attractive part. To appreciate the beauties of Rochester one must drive through its broad and shady avenues, stroll in its parks, gaze upon its waterfalls, enter its elegant public and private buildings.

BATAVIA.

We must devote a little more space to Batavia, for various reasons. It is the chief town in Genesee county, as it formerly was of the whole Genesee district, always celebrated for its fine wheat. Batavia is a flourishing and very handsome village, of nearly three thousand inhabitants. Its principal streets are built up with neat, tasteful, and in many cases, elegant houses, surrounded with trees and shrubbery. The main street is one of the handsomest avenues to be found in any village in Western New York. It is broad, straight, with double rows of trees, and forms one of the finest drives imaginable. The village, with the surrounding country, was settled in 1798, by JOSEPH ELLICOTT, BENJAMIN ELLICOTT, JAMES BRISBANE, J. W. STEVENS, and others, acting as agents or employees of the HOLLAND LAND COMPANY, the owners of the soil.

In 1780, or thereabouts, Robert Morris, of Philadelphia, bought of the State of Massachusetts that part of the State of New York lying west of the Genesee River, containing four millions of acres. He purchased it at eleven cents an acre. Soon after Morris sent his son to Holland, who sold the land to a company for thirty-seven and a-half cents per acre. This company established an agency at Philadelphia, and a sub-agency at Batavia, with Joseph Ellicott at the head. They sold the land at from two to five dollars per acre.

The pioneers of this new country, densely covered with forests, were mostly from the New England States, hardy, intelligent and adventurous men. The early settlement was one of great activity, enterprise, hardship and indomitable will and perseverance.

Before the construction of the Erie canal, and the payment of debt on the land, the country progressed and improved slowly. Wheat often sold at twenty-five cents a bushel, and the cash capital of the people was sent abroad. Since the building of the canal and the railroads, everything has changed. Some events have transpired in the now quiet town of Batavia, which may entitle it to a historical remembrance. It was here that the first meeting to advocate the construction of the Erie canal was held. This was in 1809. James Brisbane was chairman of the meeting. The war of 1812 put a stop to the agitation of the subject; but it was renewed soon after peace was proclaimed in 1815. Joseph Ellicott, who had early advocated its construction, made some most able reports on its practicability. These reports did more than any other single act to determine its commencement. He convinced the leading men connected with the Government of the State that the project was feasible. He was a man of genius and power, and deserves to be remembered.

Another event—of less importance, but which made a great noise at the time — was the abduction of MORGAN, who published a work divulging the secrets of Freemasonry. Morgan came to Batavia to write and print his work. He made no secret of his intention, and soon an excitement began to be aroused in the community. A friend to whom we are indebted for these details, happened to be a witness of one of the acts of the drama. Coming down the principal street from an early breakfast, he saw a stage driving rapidly east with a few men in it; this was a constant occurrence, and attracted no attention. As he approached the Stage House, then kept by HINMAN HOLDEN, he observed a respectable citizen of the place, George W. Harris, gesticulating and vociferating violently. He soon learned that the stage coach contained Morgan; that some individuals of Canandaigua, among the first citizens of the town, had come with a writ to arrest him for a debt of a few dollars there owed, and take him to that place for trial. Imprisonment for debt had not then been abolished. Morgan was lodged in the Canandaigua jail, whence he was taken in the night. Since that night, his fate has remained unknown; he has never re-appeared or been heard of. Persons of veracity, claim to know that he was taken to Fort Niagara, at the mouth of the Niagara River, and there executed. It is a curious fact, that the men designated as the actors in this tragedy, all came to their end by violent deaths.

The publication of the work continued; James W. Miller was the printer; his office was set on fire, we believe more than once, but the flames were extinguished. His office was in the second story; a small cannon was placed opposite the entrance, loaded to the muzzle, and the intrepid sons of Miller declared that its contents should be emptied upon those of the mob that first entered. A civil war on a small scale arose; men armed with clubs, &c., met in numbers near the town for the purpose of attacking and demolishing Miller's office; the citizens organized and were prepared to receive them. The town was kept in a commotion until the book was out; then direct violence ceased.

BUFFALO.

We have now followed the main, direct line of the road, from Albany to Buffalo, its western terminus. Many streams of travel and business of all kinds, converge into a single current at this point, and this current flows almost exclusively over the rails of the Central. Of course we exclude the heavy freight which seeks a market through that magnificent channel of commerce, the Erie canal, during the season of navigation. Every avenue of trade is crowded, and the business which the Central is unable to transact, fills the others for a portion of the year. The accommodations of the road, both in respect to passengers and freight, are ample and complete. The main line, entering the city from the east, terminates in a capacious and admirably arranged depot; which, however, is in no respect superior to that in the western part of the town where the track running to Niagara Falls commences.

The history of the great cities of the old world, except in later years, can alone be traced by the dim light of tradition, and their origin is for the most part buried in fable In our own country, the history of cities is more readily traced, for being of recent origin and growing up during a period when the incidents of their history were written down by cotemporary chroniclers, there is little to be found which is important, that cannot be verified by the record.

We design to sketch briefly the history of the city of Buffalo, one of the wonderful developments of our time and country, as well for the amusement of the reader as to illustrate the growth and commercial importance of the place.

We shall not undertake to state from what source the city derives its name for that has been the subject of great debate, and nothing entirely satisfactory has been presented in favor of either theory. Among the distinguished names which grace the discussion is that of Ex-President Fillmore, who referred to the matter at some length in his discourse before the "Buffalo Historical Society." The city of Buffalo is situated in the county of Erie and State of New York, at the eastern extremity of Lake Erie. There is no well authenticated notice of the place earlier than 1795, when the site of the present city was visited by a French traveler, who speaks of it as a settlement of a few houses, under the name of Lake Erie. In the same year, the late Judge Porter, of Niagara Falls, who has written for the Young Men's Association of the city an interesting narrative of his pioneer visit to Buffalo Creek, speaks of the settlement as containing four or five families, approached from the village of Avon by means of an Indian trail, and the only house on that was about ten miles east of the present village of Le Roy.

After the Holland Land Company had become the owners of the tract of land known as the "Holland Purchase," their liberal system of sales, and the advantageous terms offered to settlers, induced a large immigration, and in 1801, the company laid out the village of New Amsterdam, upon the site of the present city. There was nothing, however, in the advantages of the location, or in the time, which fostered a rapid growth of the new village, and its progress was retarded by the fact that new lands and better, could be obtained nearer the cities of the eastern part of the State, and a country better inhabited, and in the long and weary route which travelers were obliged to take in order to reach Lake Erie. There was no commerce upon the lakes, lying undisturbed in their native silence and majesty, which was not monopolized by the neighboring village of Black Rock, which by means of its more favorable natural position, became from the first a formidable rival of Buffalo.

In 1808, the immigration into the West from the East, had become so large that the county of Niagara was organized by the Legislature. The villagers, elated by the growth of the place, and the prospect for the future, which had become more flattering, changed the name New Amsterdam to that of Buffalo. The business of the village steadily increased; new traders came to the place; stores were built, shops opened, and the commerce of the lakes had its origin in the few vessels that were loaded or were discharged of their cargoes at "Bird Island," in the Niagara river, on which there was a rude store house. That island has now disappeared from the surface of the river, but forms a part of the western terminus of the pier running to Squaw Island.

On the 30th day of December, 1813, a large force of British troops, with Indian auxiliaries, crossed the river at Black Rock, took possession of the village of Buffalo, and burnt it, despite the resistance of the inhabitants. But two dwellings were left unconsumed, one of which now forms the rear part of a store, No. 360 Main street. It was then the residence of Margaret St. John. The inhabitants were driven in mid winter from their homes; some of them were captured, and the remainder found shelter in the adjoining villages. The re-building of the place was not commenced until 1815.

In May, 1816, a new charter was passed, and the first election of Trustees was immediately held. The first tax imposed in the village, was by vote of the Trustees, on the 11th day of November, 1816, and amounted to fourteen hundred dollars. In 1817, the taxable property of the village was valued at about $134,000. The year 1822 is distinguished in the annals of the city for the re-enactment of the village charter, and the adoption of a corporate seal, and the first corporate notice of the Harbor of Buffalo. The seal was changed in July, 1826, and the device, a ship or vessel, a section of the canal, a canal boat and horses drawing the same; and around the periphery or the circle, the words "corporate seal," and at the bottom, "Buffalo," was afterwards adopted by the common council, and is now the seal of the city of Buffalo.

In the year 1822, the new village was languishing and the inhabitants were about to despair of success, when the effectual prosecution of the Erie canal revived their hopes and gave a new impulse to their energies. Buffalo owes its early growth and prosperity to this great public work, and we wish it were possible for us to introduce into our sketch the history of the struggle which was for a long period carried on between the rival villages of Black Rock and Buffalo, upon the question of the western terminus of the canal; and we should be glad also to sketch the character of the leading gentlemen who represented the rival places. The limits permitted to us in this paper, do not allow that, and it must be reserved for the future historian of Buffalo to narrate that controversy.

In 1822 the village of Buffalo contained between four and five hundred buildings, and the census of January of that year states the number of its inhabitants at two thousand four hundred and twelve; and the village of Black Rock contained one thousand and thirty-nine inhabitants.

The dispute between the villages ended in the selection of Buffalo as the western terminus of the canal, and from that time her prosperity has been certain, increasing every year, until it has attained its present great size and commercial importance. In 1824-5, the shipping belonging to the port of Buffalo was upwards of one thousand and fifty tons, consisting of one steamboat, the Superior, of three hundred and forty-six tons burthen; one brig, eight schooners, one sloop, and four transportation boats, averaging over twenty-five tons each. There were about sixty sail owned upon Lake Erie, forty-two of which entered Buffalo in 1824; and there were that season two hundred and eighty-six arrivals, and as many clearances. The Superior ran between Buffalo and Detroit every eight or nine days. The first steamboat on the lake was the Walk-in-the-Water, built at Black Rock in 1822, and was soon afterwards wrecked in the bay above the lighthouse, during a heavy gale. It would require a volume to give a history of the commerce of Buffalo, from the humble beginning to which we have referred, through the years of its growth, until now, when it requires millions of tons to transport its burthens, and thousands of active men to conduct it successfully. Its demands upon our harbor room made it necessary in the year 1847, to take measures for its enlargement, which resulted, ultimately, though not immediately, in the construction of the Ohio and Erie Basins, and the Main and Hamburgh street canal. In addition to those, the Blackwell has been built and completed; and all of them do not yet afford adequate room for our growing commerce. Railroads have changed the character of the lake commerce. The old fashioned side wheel steamboat has been driven from the lakes, for the most part, and in their place, more as carriers of burthen than of passengers, though fitted for both, we have the propeller, and the sail vessel, which comprises brigantines, barques, and schooners of a size large enough to have been the ocean going marine of the last century. Not a few of them have visited Europe, freighted with grain, and returned with cargoes assorted for markets on the lakes. In 1846, there were in commission on the upper lakes, sixty-four steamboats, and only twenty-one propellers; while in 1861, the register of Buffalo showed only nine steamboats, (of which five were ferry boats, and four were laid up) while the list of propellers owned in Buffalo was forty-eight in number. Nearly all the shipping of the upper lakes is tributary to Buffalo, of which in 1861 there were eleven hundred and eighty-six vessels, comprising all descriptions of lake going craft. Instead of the old and laborious system of unloading grain vessels by manual labor, there are now about twenty elevators upon Buffalo harbor, at any one of which a vessel may be discharged of her cargo on the day of her arrival, and despatched upon another voyage.

Railroads enter the city from the east and from the west, while the Lake Huron railroad runs through Western Canada, crossing the Niagara by means of a steam bridge, brings its cars and freight directly into the heart of the city.

No city in the land is so proudly situated, being on high ground, sloping gently to the lake, affording an opportunity for drainage, which has been seized upon and improved. Probably there is not a city of its size more thoroughly well drained.

This notice, at best desultory and imperfect, must be brought to a close. The city which it attempts to describe, is now growing greater under the influence of the propitious and fostering commerce which has made it the greatest grain port in the world. Under the influence of this commerce, and the success of the manufacturing interest which is rapidly increasing, Buffalo is destined to occupy a most important and influential position among the cities of the North, as she now does among her sister cities in the State of New York. The country immediately around the city is rapidly growing better under the hand of the agriculturist.

We have now followed the main line of the road from Albany to Buffalo. Our next movement is down the line to Niagara Falls, and thence to Lewiston. We shall then return to the eastern extremity of the Central, in order to traverse the several branches, beginning with the track from Troy to Schenectady.

The region of country lying along the Niagara river, the most remarkable stream of water in the world, although its length is not more than thirty miles, has been the scene of more stirring events during the last hundred years, than any other of the same extent in Western New York. We can only glance at a few of them, in following the railroad from Buffalo to Lewiston, at the head of navigation of Lake Ontario. Many remarkable features of the river are visible from the cars, which with the wild and romantic scenery on its banks, conspire to render the ride one of the most interesting that can be imagined.

Proceeding down the road about two miles, we come to Black Rock

Ferry, a station where passengers bound for Canada leave the cars. Black Rock, formerly a village of some note, was included in the city limits of Buffalo about ten years ago. A mile below the Ferry, the road crosses a sluggish stream known as "Sca-ja-quad-dy Creek." This stream runs through what was formerly the lower village of Black Rock, and enters the Niagara river near the foot of Squaw Island. During the war of 1812, it became quite noted as being the place where the largest number of the vessels composing Com. Perry's fleet were fitted out, and for an important battle fought near its mouth in 1814. Soon after the declaration of war in 1812, the British having a naval force and the command of Lake Erie, the few American vessels then upon the lake had to retire. Some four or five of them ran into this creek as their only place of safety. During the fall of 1812, they were purchased by the Government, and in the following winter were fitted for war purposes. In October of that year, a party of seamen in boats, under the command of Lt. Elliot, crossed over the foot of the lake from Buffalo creek to Fort Erie, surprised and captured the brigs "Adams" and "Caledonia." The former was an American vessel which had been surrendered by General Hull at Detroit, in August. The day before her capture by Lieut. Elliot, she had arrived from Detroit with a few American prisoners on board; the other was a British vessel, with a full cargo of furs and peltries.

After the capture, the night being dark, in taking the vessels down the river, the Adams run aground on the outer side of, and near the head of Squaw Island. Here the American party left her, and in a short time she was again in possession of a British force; they were soon driven off, and finding it impossible to get afloat, she was destroyed. The Caledonia and her cargo of furs were saved. This vessel was added to the others in the creek, and fitted out as a war vessel. To protect these vessels while fitting out, a large battery, called the "sailors' battery," and a strong wooden block house, were constructed on the rise of ground quite close to the present iron works.

In the spring of 1813, on the 27th of May, Fort George, at the mouth of the Niagara river, was captured, and a few days afterwards Col. Preston passed over the river from Black Rock, and took possession of Fort Erie. This enabled the vessels, five in number in this creek, to pass into the Niagara river, where, after waiting a few days, a fair wind took them up the rapids into the lake and on to Erie, where they joined Com. Perry, who, with the aid of these vessels, fought the celebrated battle of Lake Erie, on the 10th of September following.

In July, 1813, a party of British troops, nearly three hundred in number, crossed over the Niagara river and landed on the American shore below the foot of Squaw Island. They soon passed the bridge over this creek and got possession of the block house, which they burned. Finding nothing to obstruct them, they passed on and captured the village of Black Rock, and then proceeded on their way towards Buffalo, as far as the high ground where the horse railroad stables now stand. Here they came to a halt. They were soon after attacked by a small force hastily collected, composed of about one hundred regular soldiers, thirty Indians, and a company of militia from Buffalo; after a short but spirited contest, the British were defeated, their commander, Col. Bishop, wounded, Capt. Saunders taken prisoner, with a further loss of killed and wounded.

In the month of August, 1814, while the American army was shut up in Fort Erie, and closely besieged by General Drummond, their supplies of ammunition, provisions and forage were drawn from the depot at Buffalo, where were also the hospitals for the sick and wounded of our army. From this depot daily supplies were sent to Fort Erie in boats, which had to pass under the fire of British batteries to reach that place. Gen. Drummond being aware of this fact, conceived a project to break up this depot, deprive our army of its supplies, and thus compel them to surrender. With the view of carrying the project into operation and accomplishing his purpose, Col. Tucker, with about twelve hundred highly disciplined troops, were thrown across the river on the American shore, a little before daylight on the morning of the 5th of August, about half a mile below this creek. The British expedition did not expect to encounter much, if any, opposition in their march to Buffalo, which they knew was quite unguarded, there not being two hundred and fifty soldiers in the place. They anticipated an easy capture of Buffalo, the complete destruction of our army supplies, and the hospitals containing our sick and wounded soldiers.

But quite unexpected to them, and most fortunate for us, a small battalion of riflemen, about two hundred and fifty in number, under the command of Major Lodowick Morgan, arrived from Sacketts Harbor only a day or two before the British expedition landed on the American side of the river. Major Morgan, with his command, was stationed on this creek, the larger portion of them near where the present bridge now crosses it. He being early apprised of the landing of the enemy below him, got his command together not far from the bridge, many of the planks of which he caused to be removed. A considerable quantity of large hewn timber had been collected at this place for the construction of another block house on the spot where the one burned down the year before by the British, formerly stood. Hastily piling two or three pieces of this timber on the top of each other, behind wnich he sheltered his men, and within short rifle shot of the bridge. All the preparation he was enabled to make was done in a very short time, and he quietly awaited the approach of the enemy. The British marched up the river and came in sight of the bridge, and seeing only a feeble force to defend it, made a rapid dash to cross; but after getting upon the bridge, they found to their surprise that the planks on the opposite end had been removed, and nothing left for them to cross upon but the string pieces. Nowise daunted at the appearance of things, they dashed ahead and saw the string pieces were covered with men. At this moment Morgan opened upon them a most destructive fire, from which almost every man exposed on the string pieces was shot down, and fell into the creek. This severe check caused the enemy to retire; but being confident of their ability to pass the bridge, they made several other attempts, but with no better success, being each time driven back with a loss of many men killed and wounded; they finally gave up the attempt to cross. Unwilling, however, to give up the great purpose of the expedition, the destruction of our depot of supplies at Buffalo, they retired from the bridge to the higher ground in their rear, and commenced fighting across the creek. After a severe struggle of about three hours' duration, the enemy withdrew entirely and re-crossed to Canada, having suffered severely in killed and wounded. Major Morgan personally escaped uninjured, several of his officers were wounded, some very severely; he lost a few men killed, and a number wounded. Although Major Morgan escaped uninjured in this close, fierce and protracted encounter, in one week after, in a picket fight behind Fort Erie, he was shot in the head and expired immediately, and was the only man in his command injured.

The results of the victory of Morgan over Tucker, were many and of the highest importance. It saved the depot of army supplies at Buffalo; it preserved the means of supplying our army, sorely beset in Fort Erie; it gave time for a large militia force to assemble at Buffalo, from which a great number volunteered to go to the relief of General Brown and his army at Fort Erie. The assistance furnished to General Brown by this voluntary force, placed him in a condition to act on the offensive. On the 17th September he made his brilliant sortie — the result of which was the destruction of the enemy's batteries, block houses, cannon, and killing, wounding and capturing a large portion of the troops employed in the trenches. In a few days after, General Drummond broke up his investment of Fort Erie (which had continued from the 28th of July) and retired upon his works at Chippewa. About this time General Izard arrived with four or five thousand regular troops, and relieved General Brown in the command of the army. General Izard soon followed Gen. Drummond to Chippewa. A brigade from General Izard's army, under the command of Brig. Gen. Bissell, had an encounter with about an equal force of the enemy, under the Marquis of Tweedale, on the 18th of October, at Lyons' creek, a few miles up the Chippewa or Welland river. This action closed all the fighting on the Niagara frontier. General Drummond retired from Chippewa, and General Izard fell back to Fort Erie. On the 5th of November, General Izard blew up the works of Fort Erie, and they yet remain very much in the condition he left them forty-eight years ago, and retired with his army to the American side of the river. A treaty of peace between the United States and Great Britain, was signed at Ghent on the 24th of December, 1814, and officially announced at Buffalo about the middle of February, 1815.

Tonawanda — is the principal station on the line between Buffalo and the Falls. It is a village of about twenty-five hundred inhabitants, standing on the Niagara river, with the Erie canal and Tonawanda creek running through its centre. The Canandaigua & Niagara Falls Railroad unites with the Central at this point. The manufactories of the place are quite extensive, and a large amount of lumber, principally obtained in Canada, is shipped for the East here. Tonawanda is about half way from Buffalo to the Falls. A few years ago, a considerable impulse was given to the business and general prosperity of the village by a company formed in Cleveland, with the intent of making it a depot for grain and other agricultural products brought down the lake. The object was to avoid the payment of about twelve miles of toll on the canal. Warehouses and an elevator were built, and for two or three seasons a large number of vessels came here to unload. But trade soon began to languish, the superior advantages of Buffalo more than compensating for the amount of toll saved, and now the village is nearly at a stand still.

Opposite to Tonawanda, on Grand Island, is the site of the famous Jewish city, founded some thirty years ago, under the auspices of M. M. Noah, of New York. The monument erected by Noah, and bearing an inscription in the Hebrew language, was standing after the Buffalo & Niagara Falls Railroad was constructed. But it has crumbled to the ground, as have the extensive mills built in the vicinity by the East Boston Timber Company. There was a flourishing settlement at this place known as White Haven, built when this company was in a prosperous state; but few traces of either enterprise now remain.

La Salle — six miles further down the river, the only station before you reach the Falls, is in Niagara county, on "Cayuga Creek," which was formerly the name of the place. It was changed to La Salle, in honor of the famous French traveler, who visited this region nearly two centuries ago. The first vessel that navigated Lake Erie was built here in 1678, under the direction of La Salle and Father Hennepin, a French Jesuit. The craft was of sixty tons burthen. She was towed up the river with much difficulty, the rapids opposite Black Rock being an obstacle hard to overcome. She entered Lake Erie on the 7th of August, 1679, when Te Deum was celebrated and other interesting ceremonies performed. The first voyage of "Le Griffon," as the vessel was called, had a two-fold object: she carried a company of enterprising hunters, who sought the forests beyond the lakes for the rich furs known to abound there; and she also bore La Salle, who burned with a desire to test his theory that the Mississippi had a navigable connection with the lakes. Father Hennepin, supposed to have been the first white man that ever looked upon the far-famed Falls of Niagara, was a passenger. The vessel reached Green Bay in safety; and after loading with furs and peltries, sailed on her return voyage. She was never again heard from, having undoubtedly perished with crew and cargo. Father Hennepin followed the Mississippi down to St. Louis, constantly engaged in missionary labors. We are not aware of the precise extent of La Salle's explorations. His idea was that a vessel might sail from the Gulf of Mexico to the Gulf of St. Lawrence, barring the slight obstructions in the Niagara river — a voyage now feasible enough, the Fox river improvement, the Welland canal, and the Lachine canal having removed all difficulties. This inland voyage is between 3,000 and 4,000 miles in length.

NAVY ISLAND AND SCHLOSSER.

On the bank of the river, about a mile below La Salle, stand the remains of an old wooden warehouse, on a dilapidated wharf. Unpretending as it is in appearance, and unattractive as it may be to the passing traveler, it has a history not altogether devoid of interest. On this spot events have occurred within the last twenty-five years, which endangered the peace of the country, and came near involving the United States and Great Britain in war. In fact, peace hung on a single thread on two different occasions, and nothing but disobedience of positive orders prevented an open rupture between the two countries. The first was in November, 1837, when a couple of armed British schooners, lying off Black Rock, had orders to fire upon the small steamboat Barcelona, expected up the river from Navy Island. This boat the British authorities had reason to suppose was in the service of the sympathizers with the rebels, then encamped on the island. The schooners were under the command of Capt. Drew, of the Royal Navy, and he had peremptory orders to sink the Barcelona, if she attempted to pass up the river. Gen. Scott, meanwhile, had placed a battery on the bluff near where the redoubt now stands, commanding the river for half a mile above and below the anchorage ground of the schooners, communicating to Capt. Drew his determination to sink them the moment he fired upon the Barcelona. He could have sent them to the bottom by a single discharge, beyond all question. This state of things soon became known in Buffalo, and a large number of persons had collected on the bluff to witness the same. Gen. Scott was in blood earnest, as every body saw, and the character of the orders to Drew were known. At length the Barcelona hove in sight, steaming slowly up against the powerful current of the Niagara. The crews of the schooners were sent to quarters, the guns loaded and run out, ready to open upon her. The guns of Scott's battery were aimed at the hostile vessels, only waiting for the smoke of the discharge of their broadsides to commence the work of destruction. It was a moment of breathless suspense. A single gun fired at the Barcelona would certainly have precipitated a bloody war. The encouragement which lawless persons on this side of the line had given to the rebels in Canada, had produced much bad feeling, both in the provinces and in the mother country. It was alleged, falsely as we now know, that our Government had not used proper exertions to prevent American citizens from aiding the rebellion, and Ministers were prepared to vindicate the honor of the Crown, at all hazards. But the Barcelona passed on unharmed. Drew took the responsibility of disobeying orders, and peace was preserved.

The other instance will be duly noticed in its proper place.

The rebellion in Canada, known as the Patriot War, is well known in the history of the country. Political troubles in the Provinces, which had been increasing in violence for a number of years, culminated in the fall of 1837, in an attempt at revolution and separation from the British Crown. The revolutionists, being aware that the Government had no troops in the Upper Province, availed themselves of this favorable circumstance to raise the standard of revolt. Emissaries in large numbers were sent to the American side of the river, and scattered along the entire frontier, from Ogdensburgh to Detroit, who earnestly appealed to our citizens for assistance, physically, and in any other form in which they could give it, in perfecting the freedom and independence of Canada. The appeal was made at a time most propitious to the designs of the Canadians. The large number of men employed on our lakes and canals, then just closed, and a long winter of idleness approaching; the multitude of others in our frontier cities who have no regular employment, were proper material to act upon, and became ready listeners to representations in behalf of freedom and independence to a country struggling for both. These appeals were of a character to arouse a strong sympathetic feeling; and the whole frontier was animated by a spurious patriotic furor. Men in large numbers volunteered to join the rebels—patriots as they called themselves — money, provisions, arms and ammunition, were freely given; and expeditions were fitted out and Canada invaded at several different points. Among these places Navy Island was selected as an eligible field of operations. This island lies in the Niagara river, not much more than a mile above the Falls. It was invaded early in December, under the military direction of Gen. Van Rensselaer, assisted by many of the leaders of the rebellion, who had escaped from Canada.

The old warehouse before mentioned, lies directly opposite Navy Island. and was used as a place of deposit for the supplies contributed by our people, which supplies were conveyed to the island for a considerable time in open boats; but late in December they obtained a steamboat called the Caroline, which greatly facilitated communication between the two places. The largest number of men collected on Navy Island at any time, was not more than seven or eight hundred; with a few pieces of cannon. They remained on the island over two months, and were finally removed through the agency of the Government of the United States. Immediately on the occupation of the island by the rebels, the authorities of Canada gathered a large force of militia opposite to the place, and frequent firing of cannon took place, without much injury to either side.

The steamboat Caroline had been but a few days in the service of the patriots, when the British authorities determined to destroy her. For this purpose they fitted out a boat expedition, and in the darkness of the night made their way to the warehouse where the Caroline was lying fastened to the wharf. The boats were moved with such silence and celerity that the enemy were on board and in possession before any alarm was given, and therefore no resistance was encountered. Some firing took place, from which a man named Durfee, standing on the wharf, was killed. The enemy, after getting possession of the boat, towed her into the river current and set her on fire, and she was totally destroyed. This was on the 29th of December, 1837. The killing of Durfee created an intense feeling of indignation among our citizens all along the border. It was alleged that he was merely a spectator, drawn by curiosity from the little tavern near by, to see what was the cause of the uproar — that he had just reached the wharf when he was shot dead. Matters began to assume a serious aspect. Newspapers and orators vied with each other in efforts to inflame the public mind. Our soil had been invaded, a peaceable citizen murdered in cold blood; and revenge for the national insult and the slaughtered man was the almost universal cry along the frontier. A rupture between the two countries was believed to be imminent. Our Government now seriously interested itself in the matter, and by negotiation, promises and other inducements, caused the horde of tatterdemalions, calling themselves patriots, to withdraw from Navy Island. This would have removed all difficulties between the two Governments, but for events that subsequently occurred. The blood of Durfee still cried from the ground; and for two or three years after hostilities had ceased and the hope of revolutionizing Canada had been abandoned, the determination to avenge the murder remained fixed in the minds of many of our frontier citizens. The idea was to visit the vengeance of the law upon any of the murderers of Durfee who might be caught among us. With this view a vigilant watch was maintained, and several persons from Canada visiting our side of the river on business or pleasure, were arrested on the charge of having been concerned in the outrage. These people were discharged after an investigation. But at length a man named McLeod, from Canada, made his appearance in Niagara county, and it was said boasted of having been one of the party that destroyed the Caroline.. He was immediately arrested and placed in confinement, and subsequently indicted as one of the murderers of Durfee. At this stage of the proceedings, the British Government interposed in a very decided manner, peremptorily demanding the release of McLeod, on the ground that the act of cutting out the Caroline was performed under the orders of the proper authorities, and that whether he was or was not of the party, holding him for trial was not admissible. Ministers professed their readiness to apologize for invading our soil; but they justified the destruction of the Caroline as a necessary act of self-defense, and were prepared to accept all the consequences thereof. And here was the second instance in which hostilities between the two countries were averted by the disobedience of a positive order of the Government. Admiral Lord Seymour, commanding Her Majesty's naval forces in British North America, had orders to bombard Portland, Boston, or New York, as should be most feasible, in case McLeod should be held for trial. Mr. Fox, then British Minister at Washington took the responsibility of advising a disregard of this order; but Admiral Seymour, in the exercise of a wise discretion, had determined to postpone the execution of the order until the result of the trial of McLeod should be ascertained. He was acquitted, and the matter was hushed up. John Bull professed satisfaction, because the court failed to convict the man of murder; and our Government was rejoiced to get him off their hands. But looking more closely into the affair, one cannot but admire the placable temper of the British Government. Holding McLeod to trial was the real offence. Whether he was convicted or acquitted made no difference in the character of this offence. By arresting and bringing him to trial, we asserted the right to execute him, in case he should be found guilty of the crime of murder. And the eagerness with which Ministers seized upon the circumstance of his acquittal to retreat from the position assumed when he was arrested, only goes to show that with all John Bull's bluster, and notwithstanding the genuine pluck of the old gentleman, he weighs all the consequences before going to war upon a point of honor.

The trial of McLeod was a curious affair, altogether. It took place at Utica, in the United States District Court, the jury rendering a verdict of not guilty. The important consequences that might follow the result of the trial drew large numbers of persons to Utica to witness the proceedings. But it was not a very creditable affair to the Government after all. The Federal Executive was terrified at the state of the case, and sent the Attorney General to see what could be done to enable the prisoner to evade the law; and yet it had not the power to interfere and compel his release by the State authorities. It was a complex and difficult question; and the British Government, which has never been able to comprehend the nature of the subsisting relations between the States and the central power, was badly bothered by the line of argument adopted by the Secretary of State in conducting the correspondence, which resulted in a satisfactory settlement of the matter.

The acquittal of McLeod put an end to a dangerous and all-pervading excitement on the frontier, and he returned to Canada in safety, where he soon dwindled down from a "lion" to his original insignificance. This was the finale of the Canadian rebellion, so far as any interest was taken in it by our citizens, and the affair was soon forgotten, or only remembered to be laughed at. At this distance of time from the transaction, it is difficult to appreciate the consequences of this *emeute* in Canada. When the news of the capture of Navy Island by the patriots reached London, the British funds fell to the amount of a hundred millions of dollars; and great apprehension was felt in respect to our business affairs in view of the threatening aspect of our relations with Great Britain.

THE OLD ENGLISH MESS HOUSE.

The old English landing at Schlosser, a short distance below the old warehouse, is known from a landmark which has withstood the effects of storms and fire more than one hundred years. This landmark is a very large stone chimney, around which is a small wooden building, It can readily be seen from the cars, as the railroad passes it within a short distance. Soon after the French were dispossessed of the Niagara frontier, in 1759, the English demolished the small French military works at the place long known as the French landing, near where the canal which passes around the Niagara Falls leaves the river, and constructed new ones a little over a mile further up stream.

In the old field adjoining Gill creek, and about half a mile below its entrance into the Niagara river, they erected military works, consisting of block-houses and earth-works, enclosed by pickets sufficiently strong to resist any attack the Indians (who were the only enemy they had to fear) might make upon them. Below and near these works, where this chimney now stands, they erected a large wooden building, long known to the early settlers on this frontier, as "THE OLD ENGLISH MESS HOUSE." The timber used in this building had been originally gotten out by the French, while they held possession of Fort Niagara, for the purpose of erecting a Catholic church in or near that fortress. After the reduction of Fort Niagara, the timber was hauled to Schlosser, the mess house put up, and *this* chimney built within it. Near this mess house and at short distances about it, wooden block-houses and other log buildings were put up for defence and soldiers' quarters. At the principal military works near the river, about thirty rods above the mess house, and within the enclosure of the works, were other store-houses and places of deposit for military stores, and the goods and other articles passing to and from Detroit and their other western possessions. At this spot they built a wharf, the water being deeper than at the French landing below. One object in removing from the old French landing and establishing themselves higher up the river, was to avoid the strong current and shallow water between the two places. Their new locality gave them deeper water, easier access to it, and more out of the current of the river. They built a saw mill at the Falls, — being in all probability the first attempt ever made to use the immense water power there, for manufacturing purposes.

During the war of 1812, a strong force of British troops and Indians, crossed over the river at the Five Mile Meadows below Lewiston, a little after midnight, on the 19th of December, 1813. They marched upon, assailed and captured Fort Niagara, and rapidly following up their success, burned the villages of Lewiston, of Manchester at the Falls, and the old English mess house, then occupied as a tavern. A subsequent invasion by the British from Fort Erie, destroyed the villages of Buffalo and Black Rock; and the American frontier, the entire length of the Niagara river, was laid waste.

The road by which the English communicated with the landing below the Falls, now within the village of Lewiston, ran from their new depot at Schlosser to the old French landing, and then struck across the country and came out upon the river bank, near the Suspension Bridge. This round-about course considerably increased the distance between the landings at Lewiston and Schlosser. They determined to shorten it by opening a new road leading straight from Schlosser landing and intersecting the old French road near the present Suspension Bridge. The determination to open this short piece of road gave great umbrage to the Indians, who were very powerful at the time, and they remonstrated in the strongest manner. They seemed to apprehend at that early period, that if the English, who were comparatively few in number, took the liberty of making roads where they pleased in the country, they would, as soon as they acquired sufficient strength, take possession of the whole. Notwithstanding the objections of the Indians the road was opened, and about half way between Schlosser and the Suspension Bridge a stockade was constructed, the wooden pickets of which, above ground, have long since rotted, but the parts under ground could be found by digging, only a few years since, and some remains of them may be seen yet. The opening of this piece of road, less than three miles in length, against the remonstrances of the Indians, created a deep feeling of indignation in their minds against the English, and they brooded over it, determining to revenge themselves when a favorable opportunity offered.

This opportunity seemed to present itself in the year 1763, known in history as the year of the Great Pontiac war. This able Indian made the bold attempt, and with astonishing success, of forming a general confederacy amongst the Indians of the West, of Ohio, Pennsylvania and New York, for the purpose of driving the English out of the country. His plan was to make a simultaneous attack upon all the English posts from Mackinac to Erie in Pennsylvania. More than a dozen English stations were attacked, and Mackinac and four or five other places fell into their possession. Pontiac, who led the attack upon Detroit in person, defeated the English troops at Bloody Bridge, now within or near the corporation of Detroit, and drove them back into the fort. He continued to besiege the place for a considerable time, but the English receiving reinforcements from Niagara and other posts on the river, made the p'ace too strong for the Indians to capture. Pontiac broke up the siege and retired into the Indian country, where he was soon afterwards assassinated by an Indian, whom it is believed the English hired for that purpose.

The Indians residing in Western New York, aided in council and in the field by numbers of Frenchmen who had settled with the Indians after the French lost this frontier, determined to avail themselves of the opportunity afforded by the Pontiac outbreak, for joint revenge upon the English. They gathered in large force on the Niagara river, nearly half way between the Falls and Lewiston, at a place called the Devil's Hole, about one mile below the great whirlpool. Here they concealed themselves in the woods and behind a ridge of ground, and awaited the coming up of the teams (which always went together under the protection of a strong guard of soldiers) employed in transportation between the upper and lower landing.

On a bright morning the latter part of June, 1763, a large number of teams with their attendants, under the protection of a guard of soldiers, numbering in all about one hundred, started from the landing at Lewiston for Schlosser, under the direction of William Stedman, who was the superintendent of the transportation business, upon reaching the spot where the Indians and French lay concealed, a sudden and appalling Indian war whoop pealed upon their ears from the woods around them, followed by a sudden rush of the Indians and French, and immediately an indiscriminate slaughter of men and animals, and destruction of property took place.

It is said, so fiendish was the desire for spilling of blood, that the water of the little brook which runs into the Devil's Hole, became discolored with it, and from this cause acquired and yet retains the name of the "bloody run." The persons of the English were sadly mutilated, and then thrown down the steep banks into the hole, as were such of the horses and oxen as had been killed, and also the wagons and much of the property. Only two of the English party escaped: Stedman, who was mounted on a fleet horse, succeeded in extricating himself from one or two Indians who had seized his horse's bridle, and applying his spurs, rushed over the hill under a smart fire from the Indians, made his escape in the woods, and soon after reached the fort at Schlosser landing in safety. The other person saved was a drummer boy, named Matthews. On being thrown down the hole, his drum straps caught in the limbs of a tree, from which he extricated himself, descended the tree, crawled down the river and worked his way to the landing at Lewiston.

Of all the forts, block-houses, buildings, and other possessions which the English had at old Schlosser landing, more than one hundred years ago, not a vestige remains but this solitary old chimney.

NIAGARA FALLS.

The traveler usually arranges his journey so as to arrive at Niagara at a convenient hour in the morning. He then delivers himself to the disinterested care of a hackman, who drives him to such points of view as can be reached most conveniently to himself and his horses, until it is time to dress for dinner; this last being dispatched, he hurries to the cars and goes his way, deluded by the idea that he has seen Niagara Falls; and profoundly impressed by the immensity of the Cataract, the hotel bills and the hackman's charges. In truth, however, he has seen Niagara only as one sees his face in a glass; nor will it be long before he will forget what manner of place it was. Granting him the capacity to appreciate the scenery of the Falls, a week's study is not too much to educate him to a complete comprehension, even of their physical proportions. Nevertheless, dear sir, or dear madam, (as the case may be) if you will suffer us to be your "guide, philosopher and friend," we will help you to spend the short hours of a single day at Niagara, in such fashion that you shall depart somewhat wiser than you came, and so that hereafter in speaking of its scenery you shall not be reckoned by the knowing ones among those "who find it difficult to express those ideas whereof they themselves are not possessed."

Supposing then that we are approaching Niagara upon the cars, either from Rochester, Lewiston or Buffalo, you are of course very much astonished that you do n't hear the roar of the cataract; and you begin to lose faith in good old geographer Morse, who told you when a child how the Falls in his day were wont to be heard forty miles off. But a fly in a telescope will obscure a planet; and even Niagara is drowned by the rattle of the railroad car in its career, and the bawling of the porters in the depot. And yet we assure you, that more than once upon a calm afternoon we have rowed out into Lake Erie at Buffalo, twenty-two miles away, and, the wind being favorable, have distinctly heard the voice of Niagara, reduced by the distance to a gentle murmur. And now, if you will step aside from the confusion of the depot into any quiet house, you will hear the rattling windows, and a deep sub-bass as of some mighty organ, and feel the earth trembling beneath you, and will become for the first time conscious that you are at Niagara.

The first thing to do, however, on your arrival, is to get rid of the hackmen, black, yellow, brown and white, whose vociferations are enough to drown ten Niagaras: for dispose of them you must, if you would not have them following you like your shadow from dawn to dewy eve. One method is promptly to employ the first one that presents himself; another course is to assure the crowd that you were born and brought up at Niagara; a still better course, as we know by experience, is to pick up a huge stone, and with a threatening countenance, assume a hostile attitude towards the most obnoxious of the tribe.

Having in some way escaped from these tormentors, we pass down the street on foot by the International Hotel and the Cataract House, and find ourselves upon the bridge which leads to Goat Island. And we shall find some fault with you, if you are not at least an hour crossing this bridge. We beseech you to study these rapids both above and below you, foot by foot. You will not find much at Niagara which will repay you better. We shall not call your attention to the beauties of the

HORSESHOE FALL.

scenery here or elsewhere. We trust you are not so stupid as to require that. But if you are imaginative, no doubt your mind will travel up the Niagara, through the four great lakes, the many rivers which bury themselves in their depths, and the myriads of lesser streams, which, thousands of miles away, in lands yet unvisited by the white man, are at this moment hurrying towards the abyss, which, like the grave, finally swallows all alike, and sends them down through Lake Ontario and the St-Lawrence to the sea. Or, if you are of a practical turn of mind, you are wondering how it was possible to build a bridge over these rushing and boiling waters. We will tell you: the old bridge, built in 1818, was constructed by sinking a heavy timber crib filled with stone, near the bank. From this long timbers were projected, strong enough to bear the weight of men and material. Another crib was sunk at the end of the projection, and so on until Bath Island, which lies at the further extremity of the bridge, was reached. The present bridge was built in 1856. It is three hundred and sixty feet long and twenty-seven feet wide.

Before leaving the bridge, and while standing about half way across, let us call your attention to a log protruding from the river about half way between the bridge and the precipice. On the morning of July 20, 1853, Joseph Avery was seen clinging to this log. He and a friend had been sailing on the river the previous evening; the friend was never seen again. During the night the cries of a man, as if in distress, had been heard on Bath Island, but in the darkness no one could tell whence they proceeded.

Early in the morning the inhabitants of Niagara congregated upon the bridge and shores to the assistance of the unhappy man. The forenoon was consumed in vain attempts to reach him with boats sent down the current by ropes; but the boats were sunk. In the afternoon a raft was sent down and reached him. He binds himself to it; the raft is drawn slowly towards the shore; suddenly it becomes fastened upon the rocks; Avery makes frantic struggles to move it, but in vain. A ferry boat is next sent down; it approaches the raft; he loosens the cords which bind him to it; forgetting the weakness produced by the exertions and fasting of the last twenty-four hours, he springs for the ferry boat, fails to reach it, falls into the foaming current, and is carried helplessly struggling to his doom.

At Bath Island you stop to pay twenty-five cents and inscribe your name in the visitor's register. The fee serves you for the season, and is a very proper charge by the owners of the island for the use of bridges and other conveniences which they have constructed. From Bath Island on your left, you see two other islands, "The lovers' retreat" and more distant "Brig Island." We then pass a short bridge, where we will pause a few moments to take a lingering look at the rapids, and then we reach Goat Island. This island contains about sixty acres. Before any bridge was built it was occasionally visited by venturous and daring men; and received its name from the circumstance that as early as 1770 it was a pasture lot for Mr. Stedman's goats. So say the books. But who was Mr. Stedman? This question you will find answered in a preceding page, where the man's escape from the massacre at the Devil's Hole is described.

Now take with us the road to the right, and walk slowly, very slowly, stopping from time to time to drink in the various beauty which puts to shame those who speak of the naked sublimity of Niagara. For eighty rods you walk under an arch of noble forest trees; to your left spreads a delightful grove; nor to us is there anything more charming at Niagara than the vistas through the trees upon the right, disclosing every moment pleasant views of islands and flashing streams, with now and then a glimpse of the deep green river and the lower fall. We shall begin to think that Niagara possesses in you hardly a fit visitor, if you do not linger here and strive to fix in your memory some of these beautiful landscapes, whose only drawback is, that they confuse the mind by their almost infinite variety.

We have now reached the north-western corner of the island, named by some base wight "fit for barbarous caves," by the swinish appellation of "Hog's Back." From this point a path and steps lead you down the bank to a picturesque little bridge, across a small section of the river, to Luna Island. From this path you have your first grand view of the American Fall and Niagara River; and if you are fortunate in your season, of those glorious rainbows, which are hardly less famous than the Falls themselves.

And here we must impress upon you, if you would really know anything about Niagara, the importance of educating your eye so that it can

appreciate the *magnitude* of these vast cataracts, otherwise you will leave Niagara disappointed by your own want of appreciation. Such is the great width of the Falls, that an optical illusion is produced, which it requires a faithful effort of the will and of the reason to overcome. You imagine at first that the falls are a few rods in width. You then graduate the height by the width, and the result is that you have before you nothing but a magnified mill dam. But remember in the first place, that the Horse Shoe or Canadian Fall is twenty-three hundred feet in width, not much less than half a mile, and that it is one hundred and fifty-eight feet high. Get these measurements well fixed in your mind; study the Falls till you realize these great distances, and then you will be prepared to see the Falls as they are, and not the diminutive counterfeit which is presented to the uneducated sense of nine travelers out of ten.

We must spend at least an hour in and about Luna Island. If you love nature you will regret to leave this delightful spot, where the sublime and beautiful have been contending for ages for the mastery, and no one has yet been found who could say which was the winner. We must hurry back to Goat Island. We will tarry long enough, however, to show you the spot on the north edge of Luna Island where Mr. Charles Addington, in the summer of 1849, while playfully swinging the little daughter of a friend over the stream, was precipitated with his charge into the flood, and both were borne lifeless into the abyss below.

Returning to Goat Island, we take the path up the river edge till we reach the staircase erected by Nicholas Biddle, President of the United States Bank, in 1829. The bank (of the river, not of the United States) at this spot is one hundred and eighty-five feet high; the staircase itself eighty feet. The journey down and back is somewhat wearisome; not enough so, however, to daunt an enthusiastic mineralogist of our acquaintance, who, on a hot summer's day, carried a specimen of rock, weighing eighty pounds, from the river's edge up the staircase to the top of the bank; a feat which you will appreciate after you have carried yourself up, better, perhaps, than you can now.

Descending the Biddle staircase, we find at its foot two paths, one leading to the fall formed by the little stream flowing between Goat and Luna Islands; and the other leading to the Horse Shoe Fall. Both of these paths are wet, and the latter pretty rough, but they are neither slippery nor dangerous. Let us take the former first; and do not be satisfied until you have penetrated into the Cave of the Winds and bearded the fury of this, the smallest of the falls, in this very den. What you will see and feel here, you may tell to us if you can. We shall not try to tell you. We can only say that when we visit Niagara this is our first resort; because we feel that we can really comprehend this fall so diminutive as compared with the others; while at the Horse Shoe and the great American Fall, we are constantly perplexed and annoyed by the consciousness that we do not comprehend them. Return now and take the other path. If you are a true traveler, push to the edge of the river and the great cataract. He who does not see the fall from beneath, does not see it at all. Go below and give the scene one hour's faithful study, and you will know the fact, even if you cannot fully explain the reason.

Having ascended the Biddle staircase, we continue our course until we reach Terrapin Bridge, which leads to Prospect Tower, erected by Judge Porter, in 1833. From this point of Goat Island, from the bridge and from the tower, you have the finest view of the Canadian or Horse Shoe Fall, which can be obtained from above upon the American side; and are more fully impressed than perhaps at any other point, with the sea-like vastness of Niagara.

By this time, if you have faithfully done your duty, your mind and body both need rest; and we will show you were to find it, in a lovely spot, where the brain, wearied by excitement and sublimity, can refresh itself by a scene of quiet beauty, unsurpassed in our experience. Continuing our walk towards the east upon the edge of Goat Island, we come to three little islands, called the Three Sisters, between the nearest of which, called Moss Island and Goat Island, there falls a little cascade, which is to Niagara what one of Queen Mab's fairies would be to a giant. Here is something we can appreciate without an effort. Let us lie upon the grass, and while we enjoy the landscape, refresh ourselves with the lunch which he who has felt the fatigues of Niagara, is taught by "sage experience" to provide.

While quietly resting in this spot, the bathing place of Francis Abbot, the hermit, we will tell you something of what is known about him. From his family it has been learned that his father was John Abbot, a resident of Plymouth, England. As a youth he was both studious and

ENTRANCE TO CAVE OF THE WINDS.

dissipated; and while yet a young man, left England, came to America, and in the summer of 1829, took up his abode in a log house at the head of Goat Island. He lived here about two years, studious and devoted to music, with no companion but a dog. He afterwards crossed to the main land and built a hut near the American Fall, at Prospect Place or Point View, where he continued to reside until he was accidentally drowned while bathing at the foot of the ferry, on the 10th June, 1841. This is pretty much all that is known about "The Hermit," except that he was a gentleman in his manners, and a scholar in his tastes; as was well known to the few with whom he was in the habit of conversing.

But it is now past noon, and we have a hard afternoon's work before us. We pass on to the head of Goat Island, where we will pause a moment to catch a glimpse of several interesting objects. On the right bank, a mile off, is a white farm house with a large chimney, the site of old Fort Schlosser; near the Canada shore lies Navy Island; and shortly above, lies Grand Island, twelve miles long and from two to seven miles wide, where Major Noah founded the City of Ararat, as a home for the wandering tribes of Israel. But Grand Island not furnishing a very inviting field for those kinds of speculation and trade which gentlemen of the Jewish persuasion most affect. The city, we believe, was never occupied by a single member of the twelve tribes.

We continue our walk around Goat Island, and recross the bridge, after which it is worth while to spend a few moments in one of the "curiosity shops" which form a peculiar feature of the civilization of Niagara. These shops are not like that in which dwelt the old gentleman and little Nell, and which Sampson Brass and Dick Swiveller were wont to frequent; nor would they afford any satisfaction to the appetite of the antiquary. We suppose they are called curiosity shops because they have no curiosities in them, on the "*lucus a non lucendo*" principle. But they are very rich in Indian work and agates. We know of no place where either of these articles can be found so beautiful or in so great variety as in some of these shops; and it is an opportunity of knowledge and pleasure lost to pass them unvisited.

Arriving back upon the main land, we take the path down the river's edge until we come to Prospect Place, where we spend half an hour enjoying the magnificent view, here presented, of the Great American Fall, which, if you are fond of facts, you will be glad to know is nine hundred feet wide and one hundred and sixty-three feet high. A few steps below the Ferry House is Point View, which is well worth a few moments of our time. We then descend the Bank on the Ferry Railway. By no means omit this. He who does so throws away an experience and loses a sensation. We beg you, by way of enlivening the trip, to observe the distance to the bottom of the bank, no less than three hundred and sixty feet. The cable which draws the car is three hundred feet long. Of course it is barely possible that it might break, and you will observe that there are no cogs in the track or wheels to arrest your progress; so that if any accident should happen your individuality is extinguished at once, and it is hardly possible your body could be found. But do not be alarmed. Everything is perfectly safe.

Arriving at the bottom, the uninitiated take the ferry boat and cross the river at once, and thereby miss the very finest view upon the American side, and so far as we know, the most awe-inspiring spectacle which the world affords. Step with us towards the American Fall around the bottom of the railroad upon the rocks. We hope the wind blows up the river, so as to clear away the mist and give us a fair chance. But never mind the spray. You will get the worth of a hundred wettings. Climb up these rocks with us. Get as close to the Great Fall as you can. Look up and behold Niagara falling from the clouds upon your head. You feel now, if you never have felt before, how sublime and fearful Niagara is, how beside it all other cataracts are but toys and playthings. You are fascinated and spell bound. You will spend an hour here and then tear yourself away, reluctantly. In our opinion there is nothing to be seen on either side of the river which fills the imagination like the view from this spot. It is perfectly satisfactory; and will haunt and charm and glorify the memory as long as you live.

And now for the "boat across the ferry." It needs no lover eloping with Lord Ullin's daughter, nor stormy wind, nor poet's rhyme, to lend romance to your journey. Give the boatman an extra quarter, be it silver or dubious shinplaster; in "tender consideration whereof," as the chancery lawyers say, he will row you out of the usual course, up the river, as near the sheet as you deem prudent. What you will see there we will not describe. If you are not paid, call upon us, we will refund the outlay.

Arriving on the Canada side, we advise you for the first time, to take a carriage. We have a high hill to climb, and longer distances to drive. Besides the day is nearly spent and we have no time to spare. Drive first to Table Rock; now but a ruin, with hardly a trace of former glory. In July, 1818, it lost forty feet of its width and one hundred and sixty feet of its length. In 1828 three other pieces fell off. In 1829, another body broke away; and on the twenty sixth day of June, 1850, a huge mass, two hundred feet long, sixty feet wide, and one hundred feet thick, was precipitated down the bank. We will descend the stairs, walk down the pathway to as near the sheet as you can; if you have time, go under. Then, having re-ascended to the light of day, drive up the river and take a studious look at the Canadian rapids. They are very beautiful; and afford a pleasant relief to the mind fatigued by the sublimity of the Horse Shoe Fall.

The driver will suggest the propriety of your visiting Lundy's Lane; and we advise you to go. The prospect from the observatory there is as expansive as the best champagne, and the keeper gives you a minute and intelligent description of the battle, with illustrations on the spot. In driving back (we hope you have chosen an open carriage) do not fail to enjoy the views of the Falls, seen through the openings of the trees as you pass from point to point. Nothing can be more charming than these glimpses of snowy foam and translucent green which form so rich a feature of the Falls.

It is the general opinion that the Canada side affords the finest single view of Niagara Falls as a whole; but not the same variety; nor is there any other spot which combines such various charms as Goat Island. We need therefore spend but comparatively a short time in the Queen's dominions; and we will drive down the river to Suspension Bridge, admiring the scenery as we go. One of the chief features of Niagara is the narrow and deep gorge through which the imprisoned waters of four great lakes rush foaming, eddying, struggling, boiling, to Lewiston, whence in a broader and more peaceful current the weary river glides calmly on, until it falls asleep upon the peaceful breast of lake Ontario. While in this chasm the water is of a deep dull green, peculiar to this river, and forming with its savage and lofty banks a scene, which would itself be famous were it not so near Niagara. At Suspension Bridge we can dismiss our carriage. Some facts relating to this bridge are worth remembering. It was commenced in 1852, John A. Robeling, of New Jersey, being chief engineer. It is eight hundred feet between the towers. The towers are fifteen feet square at the base, and eight feet square at the top, eighty-eight feet high on the American side, seventy-eight feet high on the Canada side; the total weight of the bridge is eight hundred tons; the cables are capable of sustaining twelve thousand four hundred tons. There are more than four thousand miles of wire in the cables and ropes; on an average of 3,684 wires in each cable. But let not the beauty of this noble structure, which looks like a web shot across the river by some gigantic spider, distract us from the view we get of the Falls, nor from the rapids underneath and below us. You will hardly believe that the steamer "Maid of the Mist" was navigated through them to lake Ontario.

You must, if possible, take the time to walk from Suspension Bridge to Prospect Place, upon the bank of the river, and thence also upon the bank to your hotel or the depot. The scenery is varied and beautiful, and you catch noble views of the Falls from time to time. It is a pleasant way of reviewing the studies of the day.

"And now," as the old rhyme says, "our story's done." If you can spend a week or more at the Falls, you can see many things which we have not shown you, and the longer you stay the better you can see. But what we have indicated can be seen, and seen well, in the long hours of a single summer's day; and you will leave Niagara with some adequate conception of what it is that makes it one of the wonders of the world; and, in any event, profoundly impressed with the conviction, that you can get more tired there in any given time, than in any other place you were ever in in your life.

SUSPENSION BRIDGE.

The railway from the Falls to Lewiston runs on the bank of the Niagara all the way, with the exception of the space from the great wire bridge to the frightful chasm known as the "Devil's Hole," a distance of about two miles. The wonderful rapids, commencing at the bridge and terminating in the whirlpool, form one of the grandest spectacles in the world. The current rushes down the gorge at the rate of twenty miles an hour, presenting a mass of snow white foam all the way. At the whirlpool the river makes a right angle, running due east, and from that point to Lewiston it is a series of boiling rapids, broken at intervals by huge rocks and scant spots of comparatively smooth water, until you come to a beautiful suspension bridge thrown across to Queenston, at the point where the Great Falls were originally situated.

The village of Suspension Bridge contains about two thousand inhabitants. It is a busy, thriving place, and a railroad station of much importance. The Great Western Railway, which connects with the Central at this point, crosses the Niagara on the wire bridge, and passing through several handsome cities and villages in Canada, terminates at Windsor, opposite Detroit.

The branch of the Central, from Rochester to the Bridge, which we shall notice in another place, is seventy-seven miles in length.

The scenery observable from the cars going from the Falls to Lewiston, is unequalled for grandeur and sublimity. For a considerable portion of the way you are on the verge of a frightful precipice, with the dashing and roaring Niagara two hundred feet below; but the solidity of the road bed and the perfection of the track, impart a feeling of perfect security. On the Canada side, in full view from the cars, towers the beautiful shaft erected to the memory of General Brock, who fell in the battle of Queenston. The view from the Lewiston Bridge is of the most striking and impressive character. The bridge is sixty feet above the water. Looking up stream, you are struck with the wild torrent, tumbling down between harsh and rugged banks, becoming gradually less rough, until it subsides into the broad, smooth river, gliding still with a strong current, and finally losing itself in Lake Ontario about six miles distant.

LEWISTON—is a pretty village of about twelve hundred inhabitants. During the season of navigation lines of steamboats run from this place to Toronto and to Ogdensburgh.

TROY

May be classed among the large inland cities of the State, and in many respects, it is not the least remarkable of them. It stands at the head of sloop and steamboat navigation on the Hudson, six miles above Albany.

It is the capital of Rensselaer county, and a well built, handsome and thriving town, of about forty thousand inhabitants. The prosperity of Troy has long been retarded by a sort of morbid, insane jealousy of Albany, with which its citizens are afflicted; but the malady seems to be yielding to a common sense treatment, and we may look for a complete recovery in process of time. The machine and iron works of Troy constitute the most noticeable feature of its trade and business. They employ in the aggregate not less than three thousand men. The educational and other public institutions of the city, are numerous and well supported. The Female Seminary, conducted by Mr. and Mrs. Willard for many years, has long enjoyed a reputation inferior to that of no other establishment of the kind in the country. This institution was commenced in the beautiful village of Middlebury, Vermont, in 1813, and some six years afterwards it was removed to Waterford, and soon after to Troy, where it has flourished for more than forty years. Upwards of seven thousand young ladies have received their education here, a large portion of them being among the first gentlewomen of the country. The University, situate on Mount Ida, overlooking the city; the Polytechnic Institute, endowed by Stephen Van Rensselaer, established for the purpose of instruction in the higher mathematics, and their application to civil engineering and the natural sciences; the Lyceum of Natural History; the Young Men's Association; and several philanthropic and benevolent institutions, are all in a thriving condition, and constantly accomplishing much good.

In short, Troy has all the attributes of a finished modern city, with its multitudinous churches, its well paved and lighted streets, its extensive water works, &c., &c.

It is an important railroad station, as well. The Hudson River Railroad has its northern terminus at Troy. The Northern road, running into Vermont; the Troy & Whitehall road, a link in the line from New York to Montreal; and the Rensselaer & Saratoga road, with the Central, have a common depot here, and a very spacious and suitable structure it is. The route to Saratoga, passing through Waterford, Mechanicsville and Ballston, is crowded with passengers during the pleasure season; and this brings us to speak of the most famous watering place on this continent, to wit:

WHITE SULPHUR SPRINGS, SARATOGA LAKE.

SARATOGA SPRINGS.

The name of this celebrated Spa is said to be of Indian origin, and means, literally, the salt place or spring. The Kayaderrosseras patent includes it, and embraces a large proportion of the county of Saratoga. In 1683, when the county of Albany was organized, it included the township of Saratoga; and in 1791, one hundred and eight years afterwards, it became a part of the new county of the same name. Its boundary is the river on the east, the Saratoga lake on the west, while the Fish creek, meandering from this lake to Schuylerville, encloses it on the other sides. Throughout this region, every step of the way has the most interesting revolutionary associations, now well preserved and illustrated by Mr. Lossing in his Pictorial History.

These mineral springs, it is said, were visited by Sir William Johnson at an early day, he being the first white man who ever saw them and applied their remedial powers; and the High Rock spring, which from its peculiarity was first noticed by the natives themselves, was the fountain which restored him to health. In 1773 their fame became so well established, that attempts were even then made to build in their neighborhood for the purpose of settlement; and in 1774, one John Arnold, an adventurer from Rhode Island, where his name still reputably survives, came up from Albany to Stillwater, there crossed to the lake, thence paddled in a canoe to the mouth of the Kayaderrosseras, followed it up two miles, loaded, and with his pack on his back and his family trudging after him, made his way by a trail to Saratoga, found the High Rock and the ruins of a cabin erected the previous year, improved it and opened it as a tavern. Disappointed, however, in the result of the experiment, he abandoned the business after the second summer, and was succeeded by a person of the name of Norton. The revolution breaking out, he became alarmed, left the place, joined the British army, and soon after died. A son of his, in 1783, returned and took possession of the property, but sold out to others who persevered in making improvements, in the confidence of future success. Various changes of proprietorship occurred, but the real pioneer and hero of Saratoga was a Massachusetts man of the name of Gideon Putnam, who, after experiencing the various vicissitudes and trials of an emigrant, found his way from Vermont to Bemis Flats, and thence to the Springs in 1789. The prosperous career of Mr. Putnam, in his various industrial pursuits, would furnish full materials for a most interesting biography, as well as a memoir of the progress of the settlement itself. His industry, sagacity and perseverance fina. culminated in the ownership of a large landed estate, and the erection, in 1802, of the Union Hall, then a structure of seventy feet, and still remaining as a part of the noble pile which now measures on its three fronts more than six hundred and fifty feet. But even then it was in the midst of a forest, and there are gentlemen still alive and in the vigor of health, who have killed game on the site of the present Congress Hall, from the front door of the old Union. In 1806, Mr. Putnam tubed the present Washington spring, and soon after the Columbia. As Ballston was of early settlement, and its mineral springs were known to the whites in 1772, and indeed a house of entertainment was in that year erected by a Mr. Douglass, for invalids and other guests, it became a custom for the visitors at the former place to drive over a rough wagon way to Saratoga to taste the newly discovered spring, dine at Putnam's, and return to their quarters in the afternoon. Bathing houses were next constructed, the Hamilton spring was tubed, and Congress Hall commenced in 1812.

Congress spring, however, was discovered soon after the High Rock became frequented. It was found in 1792 by three gentlemen who were shooting in the neighborhood, one of them no less a personage than John Taylor Gilman, a member of Congress, and afterwards Governor of New Hampshire. They observed a small stream of water issuing from an aperture in the side of a rock, the face of which formed the border of the brook, and on testing it ascertained its mineral qualities and pungent properties. It was situated a few feet west of the spring which is now used. By universal consent it was named the Congress spring. At that time the water came through a small aperture in the side of a calcareous rock, about eighteen inches from the ground; here it was caught in tumblers, and in this way it was obtained and drank for years afterwards. Such however, was the crowd of visitors that the supply became insufficient, and by some awkward attempts to obtain a large quantity, the spring itself was lost, and for a time supposed to be irretrievably so. But Mr. Putnam, the same intelligent person whose enterprise we have alluded to, undertook to ascertain the nature of the difficulty. After close observation, he discovered bubbles of gas coming up through the water in the middle of the brook. "I have found it," exclaimed he in the words of the ancient philosopher, and he at once proceeded to turn the brook from its channel, excavated the bed bubbleward, for about eight feet, and at once discovered a strong mineral water issuing out of a conglomera'e of marl, rounded pebbles and coarse gravel. He immediately tubed it with strong plank ten inches square, replaced the earth around it, and from thence we have continued to receive this delightful beverage ever since.

The Empire, Columbian and some other springs here, are much used, each differing from the other in medicinal properties.

THE ROUTINE OF THE SPA.

Our American watering places are like themselves only. "None but themselves can be their parallel." The Spas of Germany have an *entourage*, entirely different, and their habits of society are very much gauged by its official and social rank. At our own, it is a full dress circle where all may enter on terms of perfect equality, if *they have the tickets*, and these may *be purchased at the door.*

The first thing to be done in the morning if the weather is pleasant, is to visit Congress spring, sheltered by a modest little temple of a classic model, with a marble floor Here amidst a group of elegantly dressed but deshabilled ladies, with the blush of the morning on their cheeks, attended by solid, well to do, well dressed and pleasant old fellows, or dapper youth just let loose into society, or quite middle aged philosophic looking men, who have come on to pay the bills and look after their wives' luggage. Here you get your tumbler of the water, dipped up by an Irish lad to the manner born, who distributes his favors with much adroitness to those who have taught him the color of their money on former occasions. It is amusing to witness the delay which occurs with some persons, who are waiting their turn. The dippers well know who is who, and act accordingly, for all they get for watering the thousands at the spring, is their own, and they have no other remuneration. Pleasant are the meetings at these morning potations; friends jostle each other before they know it. Bless my soul, are you here too? When did you arrive? Meantime the band, perched in their summer orchestra, pour forth the finest morceaux from the latest operas, and the groups, when saturated sufficiently, proceed to promenade through the very pretty grounds laid out in the adjacent wood. A vast improvement this from what it was in former days. In a short time breakfast awaits the appetising pedestrians, who return to their hotels, allowed by the rules of the proprietors to choose their own time between eight and ten o'clock in which to break their fast. These meals are bountiful and refreshing. The finest hot bread and rolls, raised by the carbonic acid of the spring water, the sweetest of butter, the freshest of milk and eggs, of fish, of delicate entrees and crispy potatoes, with coffee of unimpeachable flavor make up the meal, and dispose every one to amiability. Friendships often commence in the half hour after breakfast, and become devotion by bed time. A stroll in the village to the numerous shops in which the surplus fabrics of the New York fashion dealers are displayed to good effect; a walk perhaps to the High Rock, that wonder of all new comers; or a lounge in the drawing room, where some clever girl fresh from Millet or Barilli, performs her last pieces to the delight of *pere et mere*, fill up the morning hours, varied perhaps by a game of crochet, the last pretty amusement of France for ladies in the country.

Then comes the preparation for the dinner, and the duties of the toilet, "sweet and long," and finally at an early hour, for this is the healthful custom of Saratoga, at innumerable well served tables and in immense halls constructed for the purpose, a thousand people may sit down at each of the large houses and make themselves comfortable over deliciously cooked viands, washed down with the choicest of the wines of Europe, Asia, Africa and America. And this is literally true. No better in the world are anywhere drank, than at the United States, the Union, Congress, and the Clarendon. This scene of physical enjoyment lasts for an hour or two, though it must be admitted that a large proportion of American eaters are literally "early risers"—from the dinner table. But there are always groups who linger around the board, and "seem loath to depart." From the dessert, always neat and well chosen, the crowd repair to the lawns in the rear of the Hotels, or to the spacious piazzas to listen to the music, where another hour or two is passed by groups of pleased listeners, while the young children tumble about in the grass and tread upon every body's toes. Others again take to their carriages, or to their saddle horses, and repair to the lake to spend the afternoon. This sheet of water never tires. It is a noble picture, beautifully set in a frame of Nature's best designing, alive with boats, or stirred up by the waves from the swift little steamers as they speed along filled with cargoes rich and rare, of youth and beauty.

On the colline which overlooks this lovely expanse is a refreshment all piazzed and shaded, and cool with ice creams and jellies. And as the sun begins to shed its last rays, the crowds betake themselves to their vehicles and steeds, and dust each other on the road back to the Spa. Then comes the evening meal, the *tertium quid*, the cup that cheers but not inebriates, and darkness steals over the village, and the lights of the hotels appear, a grand illumination.

The drawing rooms are again crowded, and when the evenings are warm, the piazzas are also filled, and the rustling of fans is like the noise of many waters. Presently the sound of music is heard, the evening hop, or more formal ball of subscription begins; the children always — an institution in American society — are allowed to romp first and last until bedtime, when they are dragged off by their nurses, much against their will. Then the young ladies take the floor, dancing with younger brothers, or their fashionable acquaintances, till eleven o'clock, or twelve perhaps, when a few brief adieus in the parlors, or wherever they may be convenient, are made among friends, and they separate for the nigh

On the "Auburn Road," as the original track from Syracuse to Rochester is called, is

AUBURN.

The only city and chief town of Cayuga county, is a handsome, thriving place, containing upwards of thirteen thousand inhabitants. The Owasco Outlet runs through its centre, with a fall of more than a hundred feet, affording sufficient water power for the large manufacturing business here prosecuted. The first settlement was made here by John Hardenburgh, in 1793, and it was called "Hardenburgh Corners," until 1805, when the name was changed to Auburn. The surrounding country is rich in agricultural productions, and the whole country is variegated by hill and dale, without abrupt or large elevations in any section. On the west it is bounded by that beautiful sheet of water known as Cayuga Lake, upon whose picturesque banks stand several of the most charming villages in the State.

Auburn was incorporated as a city in 1848. It has ten churches, and extensive manufactories of almost every description. The public buildings are tasteful and substantial, embracing a Court House, Academy, Theological Seminary, Orphan Asylum, State Prison, Asylum for Lunatic Convicts, and school houses sufficient for the education of three thousand children.

The Court House was built upwards of fifty years ago. At the organization of the county in 1799, Seneca county was included in Cayuga, and the judicial seat was erected on the site of the village of Aurora, on the eastern shore of the lake. The structure was of the most primitive kind, being nothing more than a roof of brushwood, supported by poles cut from the neighboring forests—the contrast between the present court house and such accommodations indicating the progress in civilization which has taken place in that region within the last half century.

The Academy is an institution of considerable repute. It was established in 1811, when Auburn was a mere hamlet, and has borne a high character ever since it was founded.

The Theological Seminary is a Presbyterian institution, established by the Genesee Synod.

The Orphan Asylum, is supported by private benefactions, and by appropriations from the county and State.

The Prison, one of the three belonging to the State, stands on the northern bank of the Owasco Outlet, covering, with the offices and yard, about ten acres of ground. The building cost three hundred thousand dollars, exclusive of the labor of the convicts employed in its erection. The number of prisoners averages about eight hundred.

The Asylum for Lunatic Convicts stands on the ground formerly used as the prison garden, in extent about ten acres.

Auburn has a cemetery, occupying a site of much interest to those who are curious in the traditionary lore of the Indians It stands upon an artificial eminence, supposed to have been the work of a race who lived in the country anterior to its occupancy by the Indians. The red men called them the "Mound Builders."

GENEVA.

Seneca is the largest town in the county of Ontario, and Geneva is the largest village, although Canandaigua is the county seat. Geneva is one of the most beautiful places in the country. It lies on the left bank of Seneca Lake, near its foot — a charming site, commanding a view of the whole of that fine sheet of water and the surrounding country, which is distinguished alike for fertility and picturesque beauty. The main street of the village runs parallel with the shore of the lake, and many of the handsome residences of the wealthy citizens have gardens attached, which are terraced down to the shore, a declivity of nearly a hundred feet. The village was not incorporated until 1806, but the neighborhood was settled at an early day. The Rev. Samuel Kirkland visited the shores of the lake, on a mission to the Indians, in 1765. The most interesting feature of the village is the Hobart Free College, so called from its chief promoter, Bishop Hobart. Education is free to all in this excellent institution, no charge being made either for tuition or room.

Oak's Corners—is the next station west of Geneva, and about four miles distant, a small hamlet containing about eighty inhabitants.

Phelps—so called from Oliver Phelps, one of the firm of Phelps & Gorham, who bought a large tract of land in this region about seventy-five years ago, lies three miles further west, on Flint creek, near its junction with Canandaigua outlet. The village contains fifteen hundred inhabitants. The town, which was formerly named Vienna, has a population of nearly six thousand.

CLIFTON.

Clifton, or Clifton Springs—four miles from Phelps, is a small village of four hundred inhabitants. The place is noted for its medicinal springs, and a large hydropathic establishment, where hundreds of patients, afflicted with every ailment, real and imaginary, are soaked and packed, week after week, some improving and others growing worse under the treatment; but all flattering themselves that their ultimate cure is certain. People may well differ in their opinion of the efficacy of the water cure. Poor Lamb detested water, on account of its flavor. He said it had tasted of sinners ever since the Flood. And then he had no faith in its curative properties. The first experiment was made in Noah's time, and he had always understood that it killed more than it cured. The system, as practiced at Clifton, has its advantages, undoubtedly. It cleans the patient up thoroughly; it enforces a rigid and wholesome diet, and secures habits of perfect regularity; while the sensible and discreet head of the institution encourages all kinds of amusements as promotive of cheerfulness and good nature. The situation of the Water Cure is all that could be desired. The buildings stand on a living stream which descends from the adjacent hills, in close proximity to the charming grove, in the midst of which the sulphur springs are found. In the summer Clifton is a place of considerable resort for pleasure seekers, as well as those in search of health. The Spa House was built more than half a century ago, when the springs, then gushing out from the borders of a wild marsh and tangled forest, were visited by persons from the surrounding country, who were afflicted with bilious or cutaneous disorders. It has been enlarged and improved within a few years, and although not remarkable either for its table or accommodations, is a tolerable stopping place for travelers on the wing. The glory of the spot is the noble old grove, through which you pass in going from the hotel to the Water Cure, the gymnasium, the springs and the bath houses. Below the grove, and many feet lower than the mineral fountains, is a broad marsh, through which the stream above alluded to flows, the volume of water being considerably augmented by the overflow of the sulphur springs on its margin. Here it is proposed to form a lake, with an artificial island in its centre, to be planted with trees and shrubbery, and adorned with a pavilion. Around the lake is to be a circular railway, similar to that in the fairy-like Congress grounds at Saratoga, the margin to be skirted with shrubs and flowers. Should this design be executed, the scene will be one of marvelous beauty.

About five miles west of Clifton is a station called SHORTSVILLE, a neighborhood of about thirty-five dwellings and a large distillery.

CANANDAIGUA.

The most noted place in Western New York, during the latter part of the last century, is now one of the handsomest villages in the country. It is the capital of Ontario county, and was about the earliest point settled west of Utica. Phelps & Gorham, who purchased a large tract of land in this region, opened here the first land office ever established in the United States. This was in 1789. The village contains the county buildings, five churches, a State Arsenal, an Academy founded by Phelps & Gorham, in 1795, and which is still in a flourishing condition, and about five thousand inhabitants. The situation of the town is remarkable for its picturesque character. Standing on a gentle eminence, at the outlet of Canandaigua Lake, one of the finest of those beautiful sheets of water with which the centre of the State abounds, and commanding an extensive view of the lake and surrounding country, tastefully laid out and well built, one can hardly imagine a more attractive spot. Brigham Young, the famous Mormon Chief, resided here, many years, and at Fayette, in the adjoining county of Seneca, the first Mormon society was formed in 1830.

VICTOR --is the next station, a place about ten miles from Canandaigua, containing four hundred inhabitants. The Seneca Indians formerly had a considerable village near the place where Victor now stands. In 1687, the French Governor of Canada invaded the Seneca country with a force two thousand strong,consisting of sixteen hundred soldiers and four hundred Indians. A furious battle was fought, in which the French were victorious, and several Indian villages destroyed. But the next year the fierce Senecas invaded New France, as Canada was then called, and slaughtered more than a thousand of their former conquerors.

From ROCHESTER, we follow the branch to SUSPENSION BRIDGE, having first taken a run down the eight mile track to CHARLOTTE, on the bank of Lake Ontario, at the mouth of the Genesee river. This is the lake port of Rochester, although the steamers to Toronto and Ogdensburgh make their principal landing at CARTHAGE, at the foot of the lower Genesee Falls, and only touch at Charlotte, on their way up and down. The village contains only about four hundred inhabitants, but it is a place of considerable activity and business enterprise, having three ship yards, elevators, saw and planing mills, &c., &c. Sir James Yeo, who commanded the British forces on the lake during the war of 1812, and who strove so long with Commodore Chauncey for the mastery of its waters, visited the Genesee several times, but he gathered no laurels in either expedition.

Proceeding west from Rochester, we come to the towns of Brockport, Albion and Medina, large, beautiful villages—Albion particularly so—and all full of enterprise. Immense quantities of fruit are raised in this section and shipped abroad.

LOCKPORT—the capital of Niagara county, is the largest village in the State, containing upwards of thirteen thousand inhabitants. It is a place of great enterprise and business activity, its early prosperity having been caused by the Erie canal. Its growth since the construction of the railroad has proceeded with accelerated rapidity. The canal is made to overcome the acclivity of the mountain ridge, here some sixty feet in height, by means of five locks—hence the name of the village—the surplus water furnishing motive power for the extensive manufacturing establishments in operation there. As the water from the canal flows directly from Lake Erie, the supply is abundant and uniform. Indeed, the water required for this great channel of commerce for a hundred and fifty-seven miles, is drawn from that exhaustless source. The advantages

We have thus concluded our description of the most interesting places in central New York, and in guiding the Tourist in his westward journey, where he will be most interested, in the scenery as well as in comfort of traveling, let him get in the cars at Buffalo, that run along the shore of Lake Erie, through Dunkirk, Erie and Cleveland, to Chicago, St. Louis, Cincinnati or any other point in the West or South. We feel certain he will never regret his journey or experience.

We would acknowledge our obligations to the publishers of Harpers Magazine for illustrations.

/IS
ION
ANT.
1863

NICHOLSON
—
PHOTOGRAPHER

WILLIAM M. PARKS.
STOCK
BROKER
Nov 23

FIRST NATIONAL
BANK
May 22 1964

ıt!

, Banker and Broker!

, Merchant and Manufacturer!

Every City and County Treasurer!

d have one of these machines.

DERS TO

Jones & Co.,

8 Washington Street, (up stairs,) BUFFALO, N. Y.

H. W. M.
PAID
N.Y.C.R.

22

F. PHELPS & Co,
OIL & LAMP
DEPOT,
135 Jefferson Ave.
DETROIT, M.

14

PAY .... Cash'r,
OR ORDER FOR COLLECTION
ON ACCOUNT OF
UNION BANK, NEW YORK.
.... Cashier.

15

ADAMS
EXPRESS CO.
241
NEW YORK.

16

nps please give the number and style of Die.

INDIAN
TER.
ARKANSAS
KENTUCKY
PENNSYLVANIA
NORTH CAROLINA
NASHVILLE
LOUISVILLE
PHILADELPHIA
HARRISBURG
MOBILE
DIFFERENCE OF TIME.
TABLE
DISTANCES!

JONES & CO'S
EXCELSIOR STAMP

(Patented October 31, 1865.)

ACKNOWLEDGED BY ALL TO BE

The Best Canceling and Dating Machine

IN EXISTENCE:

☞ THE RIBBON MOVES WITH THE MOTION OF THE MACHINE

Always insuring a bright impression, and from which can be taken upwards of 250,000 Impressions.

This new machine has many advantages over any other Stamp in use; the Die is more easily removed and replaced than in any other machine; it is substantially made and so simple that it cannot get out of order.

PRINTS RIGHT SIDE UP!

Every Railroad and Ticket Agent!
Every Insurance Agent, Banker and Broker!
Every Merchant and Manufacturer!
Every City and County Treasurer!
in fact every business man should have one of these machines.

ADDRESS ORDERS TO

Jones & Co.,

198 Washington Street, (up stairs,) BUFFALO, N. Y.

1 — B. & L. H. R. Co. BUFFALO. Mar 31 1863 H. L. LANSING Treas.

2 — GIRARD INSURANCE CO. Nov 24 1863 PHILADA.

3 — J. LEWIS MERCHANT. Sept 26 1863 St. LOUIS, Mo.

4 — PHOTOGRAPHER HAMILTON

5 — STOCK BROKER Nov 23 1863 NEW YORK

6 — FIRST NATIONAL BANK May 23 1864 TOLEDO, O.

7 — ATLANTIC & GREAT WESTERN RAIL WAY. Sept 29 1864

8 — BUFFALO & LAKE HURON RAILWAY General Agents Office. June 23 1863 BUFFALO, N. Y.

9 — A. R. NEWMAN, DEALER IN CROCKERY, Glass Ware &c. PORTLAND, Me.

10 — ARTHUR CHRISTEY STATIONER & PAPER DEALER BUFFALO N. Y.

11 — G. W. WILLIAMS, TICKET AGENT. Nov 19 1863 Portland, Maine.

12 — M. H. W. Mar 22 1864 St. LOUIS

13 — PAYABLE IN CURRENT FUNDS AT THE PARK BANK, NEW YORK.

14 — F. PHELPS & Co. OIL & LAMP DEPOT, DETROIT, M.

15 — PAY .... Cash'r, OR ORDER FOR COLLECTION ON ACCOUNT OF UNION BANK, NEW YORK. .... Cashier.

16 — ADAMS EXPRESS CO. 241 NEW YORK.

17 — BUFFALO & LAKE HURON RAILWAY Nov 19 1863 BUFFALO AGENCY

18 — FOR DEPOSIT IN BANK OF NEW YORK TO CREDIT G. R. WHITE & Co.

19 — W. S. Feb 23 1864 BOSTON.

20 — ROCK HILL Mar 30 1864 MO.

21 — R. M. S & F. June 22 1863 ALBANY, N. Y.

22 — H. W. M. PAID N. Y. C. R.

Persons ordering Stamps please give the number and style of Die.

B. & S. L. R. R. Co.
BUFFALO.
Mar 31
1863
H. J. LANSING. Treas.

1

GIRARD
INSURANCE CO.
Nov 24 1863
PHILAD'A.

2

J. LEW
COMMISS
MERCH
Sept. 26
St. LOUIS

3

ATLANTIC & GREAT WESTERN
Sept 29
1864
RAIL WAY.

7

BUFFALO & LAKE HURON
General Agents C
June 23 18
BUFFALO, N

JON
EXCELS
ACKNOWL
The Bést Cance
IN
THE RIBBON MOVES
Always insuring a bright impression

Revised Semi-Monthly.

TIME TABLES

OF THE

PRINCIPAL RAILWAYS

IN THE

UNITED STATES AND CANADAS.

Express Trains, stopping only at the Principal Stations, printed in Bold-Face Figures, in the Condensed Tables. Way and Mail Trains are printed in common figures.

BUFFALO:
FELTON & BROTHER, PUBLISHERS.
159 Main Street.
1866.

RAILWAY INDEX.

NEW YORK CENTRAL RAILWAY.

DEAN RICHMOND, President. H. W. CHITTENDEN, Gen'l Sup't. W. L. DOYLE, Gen'l Passenger Agent.

GOING WEST.										STATIONS.	GOING EAST.									
Acc	Exp	Mail	Exp	Emg	Acc	Exp	Mail	Mail	Mls	LEAVE — ARRIVE	Mls	Acc	Mail	Exp	Acc	Exp	Mail	Exp	Exp	Exp
A. M.	A. M.	A. M.	P. M.	P. M.	P. M.	P. M.	P. M.	A. M.				A. M.	P. M.	P. M.	P. M.	P. M.	P. M.	A. M.	A. M.	A. M.
	7 15		12 40		4 20	5 50				*Troy*	21	11 00	3 15	4 35		7 50			6 30	9 50
	8 10		1 30		5 50	6 40			21	Schenectady		9 50	2 00	3 45		7 00			5 15	9 00
	7 30	9 00	1 00	1 10	5 15	6 00	11 15	12 35		*Albany*	298	10 40	2 15	4 30		7 45		1 40	6 00	9 40
		9 15		1 30	5 30					West Albany	294	10 25	2 00							
		9 30		1 50	5 45				8	Centre	289	10 10	1 45							
	8 15	9 55	1 45	2 20	6 00	6 50	12 00	1 20	17	Schenectady	281	9 50	1 25	3 45		7 00		1 00	5 15	9 00
		10 20		2 50	6 25				26	Hoffmans	272	9 27	1 00							
		10 30		3 05	6 35				30	Crane's Village	267	9 17	12 50							
	8 55	10 40		3 15	6 45		12 40		33	Amsterdam	265	9 10	12 40			6 20				8 30
		11 00		3 40	6 55				39	Tribes Hill	261	8 57	12 25							
	9 20	11 15	2 35	3 55	7 10	7 55		2 20	44	Fonda	256	8 45	12 10	2 50		5 55		12 00	4 15	
		11 30		4 15	7 20				49	Yosts	251	8 32	11 57							
		11 40		4 25	7 30				52	Sprakers	246	8 25	11 48							
	9 45	11 50	3 00	4 40	7 40	8 22			55	Palatine Bridge	243	8 16	11 40	2 28		5 27				7 47
	9 55	12 00		4 50	7 45				58	Fort Plain	240	8 08	11 30			5 20	10 20	11 25		
	10 10	12 10	3 15	5 10	8 00	8 45	1 55		64	St. Johnsville	233	7 45	11 10	1 50		5 00	10 00	11 10	3 25	7 10
		12 30		5 30	8 20				67	East Creek	231	7 35	11 00				9 40			
	10 40	12 50	3 55	5 50	8 35	9 25		3 30	74	Little Falls	223	7 20	10 45	1 30		4 35	9 15	10 50	3 00	6 50
	10 55	1 10	4 10	6 15	8 50		2 45		81	Herkimer	217	7 02	10 25			4 20	8 45			
		1 15		6 25	9 00				84	Ilion	214	6 57	10 20			4 10	8 35			
		1 25		6 35	9 05				86	Frankfort	212	6 50	10 13			4 05				
	11 30	1 50	4 40	7 00	9 30	10 15	3 20	4 15	95	arrive { *Utica* { leave	203	6 30	9 50	12 50		3 45	7 50	10 05	2 15	6 10
7 00	11 35	1 55	4 45	7 10		10 20	3 25	4 20		leave { *Utica* { arrive			9 45	12 45		3 40	7 35	10 00	2 10	6 05
7 15		2 05		7 25					99	Whitesboro'	199		9 35							
7 30		2 15		7 35					102	Oriskany	195		9 25			3 25	7 05			
8 00	12 05	2 35	5 15	8 00		10 55	4 05	4 55	109	Rome	188		9 05	12 15		3 05	6 45	9 30	1 40	5 40
7 20		2 45		8 15					111	Green's Corners	184		8 50				6 25			
8 40		3 00		8 30					118	Verona	180		8 40				6 10			
9 00	12 38	3 10		8 45		11 25	4 40		122	Oneida	175		8 30			2 35	5 50		1 10	5 15
9 20		3 20		9 00					125	Wampsville	173		8 20				5 40			
9 30		3 30		9 15					128	Canastota	170		8 13			2 23	5 30	8 5[illegible]		
9 45		3 40		9 30					131	Canaseraga	167		8 03				5 15			
9 55	1 05	3 50	6 05	9 40				5 50	123	Chittenango	164		7 55	11 25		2 07	5 05			
10 15		4 00		9 55					138	Kirkville	160		7 45				4 50			
10 30		4 10		10 05					140	Manlius	158		A. M.			1 53				
11 00	1 40	4 30	6 35	10 30		12 20	5 50	6 20	148	arr { *Syracuse* { lve	130		7 15	10 55		1 35	4 10	8 10	12 10	4 25
2 25	2 10	6 40	6 40	10 30	8 00	12 25	6 00	6 40		lve { *Syracuse* { arr		11 45	3 15	10 50		1 10	7 10	7 50	12 05	4 20
P. M.				11 12	A. M.		6 27		157	Warners	140	11 07	2 30				6 43			
3 15				11 22	9 00		6 31		160	Memphis	138	10 57	2 20				6 35			
3 40	2 50			11 44	9 25		6 47		165	Jordan	133	10 38	1 55			12 35	6 21	7 12		3 45

4 00		*via Auburn Road.*		12 05	9 45		7 00		169	Weedsport	128	10 20	1 55				6 10			
4 15			7 30	12 20	10 03	1 25	7 09	7 42	173	Port Byron	125	10 08	1 20	10 03			6 00		11 05	
4 45				12 45	10 35		7 27		180	Savannah	118	9 10	12 45				5 38			
5 10	3 35			1 10	11 05		7 44		186	Clyde	112	8 48	12 20		11 15	11 45	5 21			
5 40	3 50			1 40	11 40		8 03	8 30	193	Lyons	104	8 20	11 45		10 45	11 25	5 02	6 10		
6 05	4 00			2 00	12 05		8 18		199	Newark	99	7 55	11 00		10 25	11 15	4 45			2 40
6 40	4 20		8 35	2 30	12 40	2 43	8 37	9 05	206	Palmyra	92	7 30	10 20	8 57	9 30	11 00	4 25		9 55	
7 05					1 05		8 50		210	Macedon	87	7 10	9 55		9 10		4 10			
7 40					P. M.		9 12		219	Fairport	79	6 40	9 20		P. M.					
8 25	5 10	11 40	9 20	4 45	2 30	3 35	9 40	9 55	229	arr } *Rochester* { lve	69	6 00	8 30	8 10	8 00	10 05	3 20	4 50	9 00	1 40
	5 15		9 35	7 05	12 10	3 35		10 20		lve } { arr				7 50	11 00	9 55	5 50	4 50	8 40	1 35
	5 32			7 20	P. M.			10 33	235	Cold Water	63			7 30	10 33		5 32			
	5 42			7 48	12 53				239	Chili	59				10 05	9 25	5 05			
	5 53			8 05	1 10				243	Churchville	54				9 48	9 15	4 47			
	6 02			8 16	1 28				246	Bergen	52				9 36	9 08	4 34	4 03		
				8 25	1 35				250	West Bergen	48				9 23		4 21			
	6 20			8 37	1 50				253	Byron	41				9 10	8 52	4 07			
	6 45		10 45	9 00	2 25	5 00		11 40	261	Batavia	37			6 37	8 25	8 35	3 20	3 30	7 15	12 30
				9 15	2 50				268	Crofts	30				8 02		2 57			
	7 07			9 27	3 13				272	Corfu	25				7 40		2 35			
				9 37	3 33				278	Alden	20				7 22		2 18			
				9 45	3 45				281	Wende	17				7 10		2 07			
				9 52	3 53				282	Town Line	15				7 02		2 00			
				10 01	4 15				288	Lancaster	10				6 43		1 42			
				10 07	4 27				290	Forks							1 32			
	8 00		11 50	10 30	5 10	6 20		1 00	298	*Buffalo*				5 30	6 00	7 30	1 00	2 20	6 00	11 20
P. M.	P. M.	P. M.	P. M.	A. M.	P. M.	A. M.	A. M.	P. M.		ARRIVE LEAVE		A. M.	A. M.	A. M.	A. M.	A. M.	P. M.	P. M.	P. M.	P. M.

Buffalo, Lockport, Niagara Falls, Sus. Bridge & Lewiston Division of New York Central Railway.

BUFFALO TO LOCKPORT.							LOCKPORT TO BUFFALO.					
L'k-port	Tor. Exp	De & Chic.	Acc	L'k-port	De & Chic.	STATIONS.	Chic. & De	Chic. & De	L'k-port	Lew. Exp	De & Chic	L'k-port
A. M.	A. M.	A. M.	P. M.	P. M.	P. M.	LVE ARR	A. M.	A. M.	A. M.	P. M.	P. M.	P. M.
6 00	9 00	11 40	3 10	4 40	6 35	*Buffalo*	7 40	10 00	10 10	2 45	7 00	9 05
6 10	9 08	11 50	3 23	4 50	6 44	Ferry	7 20	9 52	10 00	2 35	6 52	8 53
6 15	9 13	11 55	3 30	4 55	6 48	Black Rock	7 10	9 47	9 55	2 30	6 38	8 47
6 35	9 30	12 10	4 05	5 20	7 05	Tonawanda	6 25	9 30	9 35	2 15	6 30	8 25
	9 46	12 25	4 32		7 20	La Salle	6 09	9 19		2 00	6 14	
	10 00	12 40	5 00		7 35	Niagara Falls	5 40	9 00		1 45	6 00	
	10 10	12 55	5 10		7 45	Susp'n Bridge	5 20	8 50		1 35	5 50	
	10 30					Lewiston				12 00		
6 55				5 35		Hall's Station			9 20			8 10
7 10				5 55		Lockport Jun			9 00			7 55
7 20				6 05		*Lockport*			8 50			7 45
A. M.	A. M.	P. M.	P. M.	P. M.	P. M.	ARR LVE	A. M.	A. M.	A. M.	P. M.	P. M.	P. M.

Batavia and Attica Branch.

GOING EAST.

Leave Attica at 8 00 A. M., and 11 30 & 6 20 P. M.
Leave Alexander, 8 10 & 11 40 A. M., and 6 40 P. M.
Arrive at Batavia at 8 30 A. M., 12 00 M., 7 00 P. M.

GOING WEST.

Leave Batavia at 9 00 A. M., and 1 00 & 7 45 P. M.
Leave Alexander, 9 20 A. M., and 1 20 & 8 05 P. M.
Arrive at Attica at 9 30 A. M., and 1 30 & 8 15 P. M.

Rochester and Charlotte Branch.

(LAKE ONTARIO.)

Leave Rochester at 8 35 A. M., 2 30 & 6 00 P. M.
Arrive Charlotte at 9 05 A. M., 3 00 & 6 30 P. M.
Leave Charlotte at 9 30 A. M., 3 45 & 7 00 P. M.
Arrive Rochester at 10 00 A. M., 4 15 & 7 30 P. M.

Rochester and Syracuse Division N. Y. Central. (Auburn Road.)

SYRACUSE TO ROCHESTER. | ROCHESTER TO SYRACUSE.

Roch Exp	Thro Fgt	N.Y. Mail	Ft & Pass	Stm Exp	Mail	Mls	STATIONS.	Mls	N.Y. Exp	Loc'l Fgt	Stm Exp	Ft & Pass	Alb. Exp	Roch Exp
A. M.	A. M.	A. M.	A. M.	P. M.	P. M.		LEAVE ARRIVE		A. M.	P. M.	P. M.	P. M.	P. M.	P. M.
	12 00	6 45	7 00	1 45	6 40		*Syracuse*	104	10 40	6 00	1 25	8 00	11 15	
							Geers	98						
		7 07	7 45	2 05	7 02	8	Camillus	96	10 17	5 20	1 03		10 50	
		7 13	7 55	2 13	7 08	10	Marcellus	94	10 11	5 10	12 58	7 08	10 40	
						13	Halfway	91						
	1 20	7 30	8 30	2 30	7 25	17	Skaneateles	87	9 55	4 40	12 40	6 20	10 20	
		7 40				21	Sennett	83		4 25				
	1 55	7 55	9 30	2 55	7 45	26	Auburn	78	9 30	4 00	12 20	5 35	9 55	
						30	Shunpike	71		3 05				
	2 45	8 30	10 25	3 25	8 25	37	Cayuga	67	9 00	2 00	11 52	4 35	9 20	
	3 05	8 45	10 55	3 40	8 42	42	Seneca Falls	62	8 45	1 30	11 38	4 05	9 05	
	3 20	8 55	11 30	3 50	8 55	45	Waterloo	59	8 35	1 05	11 30	3 50	8 55	
	3 50	9 13	12 20	4 10	9 14	52	Geneva	52	8 17	12 20	11 13	3 05	8 35	
		9 25	12 50	4 25	9 27	56	Oaks Corners	48	8 05	11 55		2 50	8 20	
	4 25	9 35	1 15	4 35	9 36	60	Phelps	44	7 55	11 40	10 53	2 40	8 10	
		9 45	1 40	4 45	9 46	64	Clifton Springs	40	7 45	11 15	10 40	2 25	7 55	
		9 58	2 10	5 00	10 00	69	Shortsville	35	7 33	10 55	10 30	2 10	7 40	
4 00	5 30	10 15	3 00	5 20	10 20	75	Canandaigua	29	7 15	10 20	10 15	1 45	7 25	10 15
		10 30	3 25	5 35	10 35	80	Farmington	24	7 00	9 40				
4 25	6 15	10 42	3 45	5 50	10 45	85	Victor	19	6 50	9 20	9 50	1 20	6 55	9 50
	6 40	10 52	4 00	6 00	10 55	89	Fishers	15	6 40	9 05		1 10	6 40	
	7 10	11 10	4 25	6 20	11 15	96	Pittsford	8	6 21	8 35	9 20	12 50	6 23	
5 15	7 45	11 30	5 00	6 45	11 40	104	*Rochester*		6 00	8 00	9 00	12 30	6 00	9 00
A. M.	A. M.	A. M.	P. M.	P. M.	P. M.		ARRIVE LEAVE		A. M.	A. M.	A. M.	P. M.	P. M.	P. M.

Trains leaving Syracuse at 12 00 & 7 00 A. M., and 1 45 P. M., connect at Rochester with trains for Buffalo. Trains leaving at 12 00 & 7 00 A. M., connect with trains for Suspension Bridre.

Trains leaving Rochester at 6 00 & 9 00 A. M., and 6 00 P. M., connect at Syracuse with trains for Albany.

☞ The 6 45 A. M. train from Syracuse, and 6 00 P. M. train from Rochester, run on Sunday.

Rochester and Niagara Falls Division N. Y. Central.

ROCHESTER TO NIAGARA FALLS. | NIAGARA FALLS TO ROCHESTER.

Exp	Acc	Mail	Acc	Exp	Exp	Mls	STATIONS.	Mls	Exp	Exp	Mail	Exp	Exp
A. M.	A. M.	A. M.	M.	P. M.	P. M.		LEAVE ARRIVE		A. M.	A. M.	P. M.	P. M.	P. M.
3 35	5 30	10 20	12 00	5 15	9 35		*Rochester*	77	7 50	9 55	4 50	8 40	1 35
						5	Gates	72					
	6 00		12 30	5 43		10	Spencerport	67		9 28	4 18		
	6 08		12 37	5 49		13	Adams Basin	64		9 22	4 12		
4 17	6 22	11 02	12 50	6 00	10 13	17	Brockport	60	7 10	9 08	4 00	7 55	12 48
	6 37		1 01	6 12		21	Holley	55		8 57	3 48	7 43	
	6 55		1 15	6 21		25	Murray	52	6 55	8 48	3 40		
4 48	7 11	11 35	1 35	6 35	10 38	31	Albion	46	6 43	8 35	3 25	7 22	12 15
	7 27		1 53	6 48		36	Knowlesville	41		8 22	3 10	7 10	
5 10	7 40	11 55	2 06	7 00		40	Medina	37	6 23	8 12	3 00	7 00	11 48
	8 00		2 20	7 11		45	Middleport	32		8 00	2 48	6 50	
	8 20	12 15	2 35	7 24	11 20	50	Gasport	27		7 48	2 35	6 37	11 20
5 50	8 37	12 30	2 50	7 40	11 32	56	Lockport	21	5 50	7 35	2 20	6 20	11 05
	8 50		2 58			59	Lockport Junction	18			2 10		10 55
	9 12		3 13	8 06		66	Sanborn	11		7 10	1 53		
6 35	9 40	1 15	3 35	8 30	12 15	75	Suspension Bridge		5 10	6 50	1 30	5 40	10 20
6 50	9 55	1 30	3 50	8 45	12 30	77	*Niagara Falls*		4 55	6 35	1 15	5 20	10 05
A. M.	A. M.	P. M.	P. M.	P. M.	P. M.		ARRIVE LEAVE		A. M.	A. M.	P. M.	P. M.	P. M.

Canandaigua, Batavia and Tonawanda Divison N. Y. Central.

CANANDAIGUA TO TONAWANDA.

Mls	STATIONS.	Mail	Acc	Fr't
	LEAVE	A. M.	P. M.	P. M.
	Canandaigua	6 00	3 45	5 25
8	East Bloomfield	6 17	4 05	5 50
12	Miller's Corners	6 30	4 15	6 10
15	West Bloomfield	6 38	4 21	6 25
18	Honeoye Falls	6 47	4 27	6 40
25	West Rush	7 10	4 40	7 10
26	G. Val. R. R. Junction	7 15	4 45	7 15
	Maxwell's			
33	Caledonia	7 35	5 10	7 50
40	Le Roy	7 55	5 40	8 25
44	Stafford	8 05	5 55	8 45
50	*Batavia* arrive	8 25	6 15	9 10
	Batavia leave		3 35	
56	East Pembroke		3 55	
63	Richville		4 10	
	Falkirk		4 15	
66	Akron		4 20	
73	Clarence Centre		4 40	
76	Transit		4 50	
79	Getzville		5 05	
	ARRIVE			
86	*Tonawanda*		5 20	
			P. M.	

TONAWANDA TO CANANDAIGUA.

Mls	STATIONS.	Acc	Fr't	Mail
	LEAVE	A. M.	A. M.	P. M.
	Tonawanda		6 35	
6	Getzville		6 55	
9	Transit		7 02	
12	Clarence Centre		7 10	
19	Akron		7 30	
	Falkirk		7 40	
22	Richville		7 50	
29	East Pembroke		8 10	
36	*Batavia* arrive		8 30	
	Batavia leave	7 20	9 00	4 20
41	Stafford	7 40	9 25	4 35
46	Le Roy	7 55	9 45	4 45
53	Caledonia	8 15	10 15	5 10
	Maxwell's			
60	G. Val. R. R. Junction	8 35	10 50	5 30
61	West Rush	8 40	10 55	5 35
67	Honeoye Falls	8 55	11 20	5 50
70	West Bloomfield	9 05	11 35	6 00
73	Miller's Corners	9 15	11 55	6 10
77	East Bloomfield	9 30	12 20	6 20
	ARRIVE			
86	*Canandaigua*	9 50	12 45	6 40
			P. M.	

New York Central Railway Connections.

At Albany, with Hudson River and Harlem Railways and Steamers for New York—and Western Railway for Boston, and Rensselaer and Saratoga R. R., for all points North and North East.

At Troy, with Troy and Boston Railway for Rutland and Boston—and Rensselaer and Saratoga Railway for Saratoga Springs, Whitehall, Rutland and Boston.

At Schenectady, with Rensselaer and Saratoga Railway for Ballston, Saratoga Springs, and all points North and East.

At Utica, with Black River and Utica Railway for Trenton Falls and Boonville.

At Rome, with Rome, Watertown and Ogdensburgh Railway for Watertown, Cape Vincent and Ogdensburgh.

At Syracuse, with Syracuse and Binghamton Railway—and Oswego and Syracuse Railway.

At Cayuga, with Steamers on the Lake.

At Geneva, with Steamers on the Lake.

At Canandaigua, with Northern Central Railway for Philadelphia, Baltimore and Washington.

At Rochester, with Genesee Valley Railway.

At Charlotte, by Steamers to all ports on Lake Ontario.

At Buffalo, with Buffalo and Erie Railway to Cleveland—Grand Trunk Railway—and Steamers on Lake Erie.

At Suspension Bridge, with Great Western Railway through Canada West to Detroit.

At Lewiston, with Lake Ontario Steamers for Toronto, Kingston, Sackett's Harbor, Cape Vincent, Ogdensburgh, Montreal and Quebec.

Through Routes by Express Passenger Trains.

GOING WEST.						STATIONS.		GOING EAST.				
A. M. 7 45	A. M. 11 00	P. M. 5 00	P. M. 7 00	P M. 11 00	LEAVE	New York	ARRIVE	P. M. 10 30	A. M 6 00	A. M. 7 00	P. M. 12 40	P. M. 3 45
						BOSTON LINE.						
A. M. 4 45	A. M. 8 03	P. M. 2 30		P. M. 8 30	Leave	Boston	Arrive	A. M. 12 15	A. M. 6 00	P. M. 3 50	P. M. 3 50	P. M. 5 00
6 15	10 05	4 00		10 00		Worcester	Leave	P. M. 10 45	4 15	2 00	2 00	3 40
8 30	P. M. 12 25	6 20		A. M. 12 20		Springfield		8 55	2 10	A. M. 11 30	A. M. 11 30	1 46
P. M. 12 40	5 25	10 50		5 25	Arrive	Albany		4 45	P. M. 9 10	6 30	6 30	A. M. 9 50
						NEW YORK CENTRAL.						
P. M 1 00	P. M. 6 00	P. M. 11 15	A. M. 12 35	A. M. 7 30	Leave	Albany	Arrive	P. M. 4 30	P. M. 7 45	A. M. 1 40	A. M. 6 00	A. M. 9 40
12 40	5 50			7 15		Troy	Leave	4 35	7 50		6 30	9 50
1 45	6 50	A. M. 12 00	1 20	8 15		Schenectady		3 45	7 00	1 00	5 15	9 00
4 45	10 20	3 25	4 20	11 35		Utica		12 50	3 45	10 05	2 15	6 10
6 40	A. M. 12 25	6 00	6 40	P. M. 1 40		Syracuse		A. M. 10 55	1 35	P. M. 8 10	12 10	4 25
10 20	4 00	3 00	10 15	5 20		Canandaigua		7 15	10 15	1 45	7 25	10 15
11 40	5 15	5 00	11 30	6 45	Arrive	Rochester		6 00	A. M. 9 00	12 30	P. M. 6 00	P. M. 9 00
P. M. 9 35	3 55	9 40	10 20	5 15	Leave	Rochester		8 10	10 05	4 50	9 00	A. M. 1 40
12 15	6 35	P. M. 1 15	P. M. 1 15	8 30	Arrive	Suspension Bridge		5 10	6 50	1 30	5 40	P M. 10 20
12 30	6 50	1 30	1 30	8 45		Niagara Falls		4 45	6 35	1 15	5 20	10 05
11 50	6 20	1 00	1 00	8 00		Buffalo		5 30	7 30	2 20	6 00	11 20
						CINCINNATI LINE						
P. M. 11 45	A. M. 6 30		P. M. 1 10	P. M. 9 00	Leave	Buffalo	Arrive	A. M. 4 50		P. M. 1 35	P. M. 5 20	P. M. 10 40
A. M. 2 55	10 10		4 25	A. M. 1 10		Erie	Leave	1 25		A. M. 10 15	2 00	7 35
5 50	P. M. 2 10		7 55	5 05	Arrive	Cleveland		P. M. 9 40		6 30	A. M. 9 50	4 00
11 30	11 00		A. M. 2 00			Columbus		1 15		P. M. 12 30		A. M. 11 00
P. M. 4 20	A. M. 4 45		6 40			Cincinnati		A. M. 8 25		8 00		7 00
						CHICAGO LINES.						
A. M 12 15	A. M. 7 00		P. M. 1 30	P. M.	Leave	Suspension Bridge	Arrive	A. M. 4 25		P. M.	P. M. 4 40	P. M. 9 25
10 30	P. M. 5 25		10 45			Detroit	Leave	P. M. 7 30			A. M. 7 30	A. M. 11 00
P. M. 11 45	A. M. 6 30		1 10	9 00		Buffalo	Arrive	A. M. 4 50		1 35	P. M. 5 20	P. M. 10 00
2 55	10 10		4 24	A. M. 1 10		Erie	Leave	1 25		A. M. 10 15	2 00	6 55
5 50	P. M. 2 40		8 30	5 05		Cleveland		P. M 9 40		6 30	A. M. 9 50	3 25
A. M. 10 45	7 40		A. M 1 10			Toledo		5 05			4 50	A. M. 10 10
9 15	6 40		12 00			Crestline		6 25			6 25	12 50
P M. 8 00	A. M. 6 00		11 30		Arrive	Chicago		A. M. 7 00			P. M. 5 30	P. M. 10 00

LAKE SHORE RAILWAY LINE.

Buffalo & Erie Railway.—D. Richmond, Pres., and J. Lewis Grant, Supt., Buffalo, N. Y.
Cleveland & Erie Railway.—A. Stone, Jr., Pres., and H. Nottingham, Supt., Cleveland, O.

Otis Kimball, General Agent, Buffalo, N. Y. John F. Porter, General Agent, 247 Broadway, New York. H. W. Carr, Western Agent, 54 Clark street, Chicago. I. J. Bassett, and H. K. Hobart, Agents, Old State House, Boston. [*July 2.*

GOING WEST.						STATIONS.	GOING EAST.					
Stm. Exp	Tol. Exp.	Day Exp.	Mail	Ni't Exp.	Mls		Mls	Cin. Exp.	Day Exp.	Mail	Ni't Exp.	N.Y. Exp.
P. M.	A. M.	P. M.	P. M.	P. M.		LEAVE — ARRIVE		P. M.	P. M.	A. M.	A. M.	P. M.
9 00	6 30	1 10	4 00	11 45		*Buffalo*	538	10 40	5 20	10 10	4 50	1 35
	6 55		4 25		10	Hamburg				9 45		
	7 09		4 40 4 46		15	North Evans	523			9 30		
9 55	7 22	2 00	5 03		21	Angola	517		4 35	9 14		12 44
	7 32		5 16		26	Farnham				9 00		
	7 40		5 25		29	Irving	509			8 51		
10 25	7 50	2 26	5 33	12 55	31	Silver Creek	507	9 33	4 10	8 41	3 35	12 20
10 50	8 15	2 50	6 00 6 10	1 15	40	arrive / leave } *Dunkirk* { leave / arrive	498	9 14	3 50 3 45	8 15	3 15	12 02
	8 35		6 38		48	Brocton	490			7 52		
	8 41		6 45		50	Portland				7 46		
11 40	9 00	3 34	7 10	1 50	57	Westfield	481	8 37	3 00	7 30	2 35	11 25
			7 26		62	Ripley Crossing				7 17		
	9 18		7 36		65	Ripley				7 10		11 05
	9 27		7 46		68	State Line				7 01	2 12	
12 25	9 40	4 05	8 05		73	North East		8 05		6 52		10 47
			8 16		77	Morehead				6 44		
	9 55		8 25		80	Harbor Creek				6 35		
			8 37		84	Wesleyville				6 20		
1 05	10 15	4 35	8 50	2 55	88	*Erie*	450	7 35	2 00	6 10	1 25	10 15
	10 37					Fairview						
1 46	10 48	5 08		3 16	103	Girard	435					
	11 00					Springfield						
2 18	11 18	5 37			115	Conneaut	423					
	11 36				123	Kingsville	415					
2 51	11 51	6 09		4 05	129	Ashtabula	409					
	12 15				138	Geneva	400					
	12 28				143	Madison	395					
3 53	12 55	7 00		4 55	154	Painesville	384					
	1 20				165	Willoughby	373					
	1 45				174	Euclid	364					
5 05	2 10	7 55	5 30	5 50	183	*Cleveland*	355					
	7 30	1 00		10 40	295	Toledo	243					
	6 00	11 30		9 30	538	Chicago	0					
	1 15	8 30		1 15		Milwaukee						
	10 50	1 50		11 30		Columbus						
	4 45	6 40		4 20		Cincinnati						
	5 10	5 10		5 20		Louisville						
	10 45	10 45		9 00		St. Louis						
A. M.	P. M.	A. M.	A. M.	A. M.		ARRIVE — LEAVE		A. M.	A. M.	P. M.	P. M.	A. M.

All Express Trains, make direct connections at Buffalo, with Express Trains on New York Central Railway, for Niagara Falls, Albany, New York, Boston, &c.

All Express Trains connect at Cleveland with Cleveland & Toledo and Cleveland, Columbus & Cincinnati Railways, for Cincinnati, Chicago, St. Louis, &c. Also connect at Cleveland, with Cleveland & Pittsburg Railway, Cleveland & Mahoning Railway and with steamers for upper Lakes.

Connect at Girard with Pittsburg & Erie Railway; at Dunkirk with Erie Railway.

NORTHERN CENTRAL RAILWAY.

Jas. D. Cameron, President; J. N. Du Barry, Gen. Supt.; J. S. Leib, Treas.; R. S. Hollins, Sec.; and E. S. Young, Gen. Freight and Passenger Agent, Baltimore. [*Aug. 5.*

GOING NORTH.							STATIONS.	GOING SOUTH.						
Har. Acc.	Mail	Fast Line	Y'rk Acc.	Erie Exp.	Buff. Exp.	Mls		Mls	Mail	Buff. Exp.	Y'rk Acc.	Fast Line	Har. Acc.	Cin. Exp.
A. M.	A. M.	A. M	P. M.	P. M.	P. M.		LEAVE ARRIVE		P. M.	A. M.	A. M.	P. M.	P M.	A. M.
	7 00	7 30		4 30	8 00		....Washington....		9 25	10 20		5 05		
	9 50	11 50		8 30	8 50		....Philadelphia....		5 40	7 00		1 00		
7 20	9 25	12 10	3 30	7 20	10 10	0	.....*Baltimore* [1].....	256	6 00	7 00	10 15	12 30		12 20
7 28	9 32	12 16	3 38	7 28	10 16	1	.......Bolton.......	255	5 55	6 52	10 07	12 24		12 14
							.....Woodberry....							
							......Melvale......							
							..Mt. Washington..							
7 45	9 5	12 31	4 00	7 46	10 28	7	.......Relay.......	249	5 30	6 35	9 43	12 02		11 57
						9	.......Rider's.......	247						
							.....Lutherville.....							
8 00	10 00	12 42	4 18	8 00	10 38	12	.....Timonium.....	244	5 15	6 23	9 25	11 52		11 47
							.......Texas.......							
8 08	10 11	12 51	4 30	8 11	10 45	15	....Cockeysville....	241	5 04	6 15	9 12	11 45		11 40
							......Ashland......							
							......Phœnix......							
8 25	10 21	1 03	4 45	8 26	10 57	20	.......Sparks'.......	236	4 48	6 02	8 58	11 31		11 26
							......Glencoe......							
							......Corbitt's......							
8 35	10 30	1 10	4 56	8 37	11 0[illegible]	23	......Monkton......	233	4 38	5 52	8 47	11 25		11 20
							....Blue Mount....							
							.....White Hall....							
8 55	10 45	1 23	5 15	8 55	11 15	29	......Parkton......	227	4 20	5 37	8 30	11 10		11 05
							......Bee Tree......							
9 15	11 02	1 38	5 35	9 15	11 28	31	.....Freeland's.....	222	4 01	5 24	8 15	10 58		10 53
9 23	11 10	1 4	5 44	9 20	1 [illegible]	36	....Summit No. 1...	220	3 55	5 17	8 07	10 52		10 47
							....Shrewsbury....							
9 44	1 27	2 00	5 58	9 35	11 47	42	......Glenrock......	214	3 35	5 00	7 50	10 40		10 33
10 00	11 44	2 12	6 12	9 50	11 55	46	.Hanover Junction [2]	210	3 20	4 43	7 35	10 25		10 20
							......Smyser's......							
10 07	11 51	2 18	6 20	9 58	12 0	49	.....Glatfelter's....	207	3 12	4 57	7 27	10 19		10 14
							......Brilhart's......							
10 35	12 15	2 40	6 50	10 25	12 25	57	arr } ..York [3]. { lve	199	2 50	4 15	7 00	10 00		9 55
10 40	12 20	2 45		10 30	12 3		lve } { arr		2 45	4 10		9 57	6 35	9 52
							.....Emigsville.....							
10 58	12 34	2 57		10 45	12 47	6[illegible]	....Summit No. 2...	[illegible]3	2 30	3 55		9 43	6 17	9 38
11 10	12 43	3 06		10 58	1[illegible]	6[illegible]	....Conewagon....	189	2 [illegible]	3 45		9 35	6 05	9 30
11 25	12 55	3 16		11 3	1 05	7[illegible]	.....Goldsboro.....	[illegible]	2 10	3 33		9 25	5 53	9 20
							.Middletown Ferry.							
11 43	1 08	3 7		11 27	1 1	7[illegible]	......Red Bank.....	178	1 58	3 20		9 13	5 37	9 07
							.New Cumberland.							
12 00	1 20	3 40		11 45	1 30	8[illegible]	arr } Bridge- { lve	17[illegible]	1 47	3 05		9 00	5 20	8 55
	2 20			12 30	2 20		lve } port [4] { arr		1 [illegible]	2 20				
12 1	1 35	3 50		12 00	1 4[illegible]	85	arr } *Harris-* { lve	175	1 35	2 50		8 47	5 05	8 40
	2 05	4 10		12 20	2 05		lve } *burg* [5] { arr		1 15	2 30		8 35		
	2 27					86	......Fairview......	170	12 53					
	2 40			1 00	2 45	91	.....Marysville.....	165	12 40	1 55				
	2 50	4 35			2 57	93	......Dauphin [6].....	163	12 30	1 45		8 05		
	3 05	4 50			3 08	99	...Clark's Ferry...	157	12 16	1 28		7 50		
	3 20	5 08			3 25	106	......Halifax......	150	11 59	1 11		7 33		
	3 35	5 23			3 40	112	....M[illegible]urg....	144	11 44	12 56		7 18		
							......Liverpool.....							
	3 50	5 38			3 57		....Mahantongo....		11 30	12 39		7 03		
	4 00	5 48			4 08	122	....Georgetown....	134	11 20	12 31		6 58		
	4 13	6 00			4 [illegible]	127	.....Trevorton.....	129	11 06	12 20		6 43		
	4 27	6 15			4 30	133	....Selin's Grove...	123	10 52	12 05		6 27		
	4 40	6 30			4 4	138	arr } *Sunbury* [7] { lve / lve } { arr	118	10 40	11 50		6 15		
P. M.	P. M.	P. M.	P. M	A. M.	A. M.		ARRIVE LEAVE		A. M.	P. M.	P. M.	A. M.	P. M.	P. M.

Northern Central Railway (continued.)

GOING NORTH.							STATIONS.	GOING SOUTH.						
Har. Acc.	Mail	Fast Line	Y'rk Acc.	Erie Exp.	Buff. Exp.	Mls		Mls	Mail	Buff. Exp.	Y'rk Acc.	Fast Line	H'rg Acc.	Cin. Exp.
P. M.	P. M.	P. M.	A. M.	A. M.	P. M.		LEAVE ARRIVE		A. M.	A. M.	A. M.	P. M.	A. M.	A. M.
	4 40	6 20			4 45	128	arr / lve *Sunbury* [7] lve / arr	118	10 40	11 50		6 15		
							Northumberland							
							Lewisburg							
							Milton							
							Watsontown							
							Dewart							
							Montgomery							
							Muncy							
	6 50	8 25			6 55	178	arr / lve *Williams-port* lve / arr	78	8 45	9 55		4 40		
						185	Cogan Valley	71						
						188	Crescent	68						
						192	Trout Run	64						
						200	Lycoming	56						
						202	*Ralston*	54						
						217	Canton	39						
						222	Alba	34						
						225	West Granville	31						
						230	Troy	26						
						235	Columbia X Roads	21						
		1 15			11 35	256	*Elmira* [8]	0		5 30		1 05		
		4 00			3 00		Canandaigua			2 00		10 20		
		5 20			5 00		Rochester			12 30		9 00		
		10 30			8 00		Buffalo			7 30		6 00		
		9 35			8 00		Niagara Falls			6 35		5 20		
		2 20			1 10		Pittsburg							
A. M.	A. M.	A. M.	P. M.	P. M	A. M.		ARRIVE LEAVE		P. M.	P. M.	P. M.	A. M.	P. M.	P. M.

[1] Connects with Baltimore & Ohio Railway, and Washington Branch.
[1] Connects with Philadelphia, Wilmington & Baltimore Railway.
[2] Connects with Hanover Branch Railway.
[3] Connects with Wrightsville, York & Columbia Railway.
[4] Connects with Cumberland Valley Railway.
[5] Connects with Pennsylvania Central Railway.
[5] Connects with Lebanon Valley Railway.
[6] Connects with Schuylkill & Susquehanna Railway.
[7] Connects with Philadelphia & Erie Railway.
[8] Connects with Erie Railway, and Elmira & Canandaigua Railway.

PARKTON TRAINS.—Trains leave Baltimore (Calvert Station) for Parkton, at 12 30 & 5 30 P. M. Returning—Leave Parkton at 6 30 A. M. and 2 45 P. M.

WRIGHTSVILLE, Y RK & COLUMBIA RAILWAY.

Leave York for Wrightsville at 6 45 A. M., and 12 10 & 3 00 P. M.
Returning—Leave Wrightsvill at 8 00 A. M., and 1 20 & 7 00 P. M. Distance 13 miles. Connects at Wrightsville with Philadelphia trains.

SHAMOKIN VALLEY & POTTSVILLE RAILWAY.

(LEASED AND RUN BY NORTHERN CENTRAL RAILWAY.)

Going West—Leaves Mt. Carmel at 7 50 A. M., arr. at Shamokin at 8 25, and Sunbury at 9 40 A. M.
Going East—Leaves Sunbury at 4 40 P. M., arr. at Shamokin at 5 55, and Mt. Carmel 6 40 P. M. Distance 28 miles.

Northern Central Railway

DIRECT SOUTHERN ROUTE!

PASSENGER AND FREIGHT LINE.

TO BALTIMORE, WASHINGTON, PHILADELPHIA,

Harrisburg, Williamsport, and all Points South!

Passenger Trains run through between ROCHESTER and BALTIMORE without change of Cars. Only one change between ROCHESTER and PHILADELPHIA or WASHINGTON.

Freight carried through from Buffalo, Suspension Bridge, or any point on New York Central *without transfer*. Only one change from points on

ERIE RAILWAY AND BALTIMORE OR PHILADELPHIA.

This route to the South offers to passengers and shippers of freight. greater advantages than those possessed by any other line, being from 100 to 200 miles shorter from Northern, Central and Western New York, than via New York City, with a corresponding reduction of fare and rates of freight, and less changes of cars. Cars loaded with freight in Buffalo. Rochester, or any point on New York Central, go through to destination without breaking bulk. Freight from points on Erie Railway is carried to destination with only one change.

The arrangements with our connections at Canandaigua with the New York Central, and at Elmira with the Erie Railway, at Watkins with Lake and Canal Navigation from points not reached by rail, are such as to enable us to guarantee to our patrons full satisfaction in time and rates of transportation.

The devastation of the Southern States by the late war, in the destruction of almost their entire stock of cereals, fruits, &c., will compel our Southern planters to seek in the North the means of renewing their stock, and this great and direct avenue, now successfully opened, offers a quick and safe transit.

RENSSELAER & SARATOGA RAILWAY.

Comprising Rensselaer & Saratoga, Albany Northern, Saratoga & Schenectady, Saratoga & Whitehall and Rutland & Washington Railways.

GEO. H. CRAMER, President. [*July* 16.] I. V. BAKER, Superintendent.

TRAINS GOING NORTH.

STATIONS.	Mls	Mail	Acc.	Exp.
		A. M.	P. M.	P. M.
Leave Albany		7 10	5 15	12 40
Schenectady		8 00	4 00	
Troy [1]		7 30	5 30	1 00
Green Island	1	7 36	5 35	1 05
Waterford	5	7 49	5 48	1 16
Albany Junction	6	7 58	5 57	1 24
Mechanicville	12	8 13	6 15	1 41
East Line		8 38	6 39	2 06
Ballston [2]	25	8 46	6 48	2 14
Saratoga { Arrive	32	9 05	7 05	2 35
Saratoga { Leave		9 20	7 15	
Gansevoorts	43	9 47	7 42	
Moreau [3]	48	10 00	7 58	
Fort Edward	49	10 05	8 05	
Dunham's Basin	52	10 13	8 13	
Smith's Basin	57	10 25	8 25	
Fort Ann	61	10 36	8 35	
Comstock's La'ding	65	10 47	8 45	
Whitehall { Junction, arr.	71	11 05	9 03	
Whitehall { L. Cham.[4] arr.	73	11 15	9 13	
Whitehall { Junction, l've		11 10	9 10	
Fairhaven	79	11 33	9 35	
Hydeville	81	11 40	9 43	
Castleton [5]	85	11 50	9 55	
West Rutland	91	12 06	10 12	
Centre Rutland	93	12 13	10 18	
Arr. at *Rutland* [6]	95	12 20	10 25	
		P. M.	P. M.	P. M.

TRAINS GOING SOUTH.

STATIONS.	Mls	Acc.	Mail	Exp.
		A. M.	P. M.	P. M.
Leave *Rutland*		5 00	2 45	
Centre Rutland	2	5 06	2 51	
West Rutland	4	5 12	2 57	
Castleton	10	5 28	3 20	
Hydevile	14	5 37	3 30	
Fairhaven	16	5 43	3 38	
Whitehall { Junction, arr.	24	6 05	4 05	
Whitehall { L. Cham. l've.	26	6 00	4 05	
Whitehall { Junction, l've.		6 10	4 15	
Comstock's La'ding	31	6 28	4 33	
Fort Ann	35	6 39	4 43	
Smith's Basin	38	6 50	4 53	
Dunham's Basin	43	7 02	5 03	
Fort Edward	46	7 13	5 12	
Moreau	47	7 19	5 20	
Gansevoorts	52	7 33	5 35	
Saratoga { Arrive	63	8 00	6 00	
Saratoga { Leave		8 10	6 10	3 00
Ballston	69	8 29	6 29	3 19
East Line		8 38	6 39	
Mechanicville	83	9 01	7 02	3 50
Albany Junction	89	9 18	7 20	4 05
Waterford	91	9 23	7 25	4 13
Green Island	94	9 35	7 40	4 25
Arr. at Troy	95	9 40	7 45	4 30
Albany		9 55	7 50	4 40
Schenectady		9 40	6 30	
		A. M.	P. M.	P. M.

[1] Connects with Hud. Riv. R'way; Troy & Schenectady R'way; Troy & Greenbush R'way.
[1] Steamboats to New York, &c.
[2] Junc. of Saratoga & Schenectady Railway.
[3] Glen's Falls, Lake George, &c.
[4] St'mboats to Burlington, Plattsb'h & Mont.
[5] Junc. of Rutland & Washington Railway.
[6] Connects with Rutland & Burlington R'way.

Rutland & Washington Division.

GOING NORTH. Mail	N Ex	Mls	STATIONS.	GOING SOUTH. Mls	N Ex	Mail
P. M.	P. M.		LEAVE ARRIVE		A. M.	P. M.
1 00	9 40		Troy		4 40	4 15
1 45	10 30		Eagle Bridge	63	3 50	3 15
1 59	10 46	6	Cambridge	57	3 38	2 58
2 11	10 58	11	Shushan	52	3 20	2 46
			Baxterville			
2 27	11 15	18	Salem	45	3 03	2 27
2 47	11 37	27	Rupert	36	2 40	2 05
3 02	11 55	34	Pawlet	29	2 23	1 49
3 09	12 03	37	Granville	26	2 15	1 41
3 14	12 08	39	Mid. Granville	24	2 10	1 36
3 28	12 23	45	Poultney	18	1 55	1 22
			Hosfords			
3 44	12 39	52	Castleton	11	1 37	1 06
4 00	1 00	59	West Rutland	4	1 20	12 50
4 05	1 05	61	Centre Rutland	2	1 15	12 45
4 10	1 10	63	Rutland		1 10	12 40
P. M.	P. M.		ARRIVE LEAVE		A. M.	P. M.

Schenectady Division.

Trains going North, leave Schenectady for Half-way House, Ballston and Saratoga, at 8 00 A. M., 4 00 and 7 20 P. M.

Going South, leave Saratoga for Ballston, Half-way House and Schenectady, at 6 15 A. M. and 6 00 P. M., connecting with trains on New York Central Railway.

Distance 22 miles.

Albany Division.

Trains going North, leave Albany for Cemetery, West Troy, Cohoes, Waterford and Junction, at 7 10 and 8 15 A. M., 12 40, 2 40 and 5 15 P. M.

Going South, leave Junction for Waterford, Cohoes, West Troy, Cemetery and Albany, at 8 05 and 9 20 A. M., 1 30, 4 00 and 7 20 P. M.

Distance 12 miles.

NORTH MISSOURI RAILWAY.

ISAAC H. STURGEON, President and Gen. Supt., St. Louis. JOHN O. FARRAR, Vice Pres. JOHN F. HUME, Fund Commissioner. HENRY OVERSTOLZ, Business Director. J. B. MOULTON, Chief Eng., St. Louis. JAS. A. FELPS, Asst. Supt. H. H. Wheeler, Gen. Ticket Agent, and W. W. EHNINGER, Gen. Freight Agent, St. Louis, Mo. R. T. Brown, Gen. Trav. Agent. [*Jan.* 19.

CONNECTIONS.

At St. Joseph, with the Platte County Railway, to Atchison, Weston, and Savannah; also, with Tri-Weekly Line of Packets and Daily Line of Stages for Nebraska City, Council Bluffs and Omaha.

At Atchison, with the Daily Overland Stages, to Denver City, Salt Lake City, the Gold Mines of Idaho and Nevada, Bannock City, Virginia City and California.

At Weston, with Daily Packets for Kansas City.

At Leavenworth City, with Daily Stage Line for Lawrence, Lecompton, Fort Riley, Santa Fe, and all points of New Mexico; also, with Tri-Weekly Line to Ossawatomie and Fort Scott.

At Omaha, with Daily Stage Line to Ft. Kearney, at which place they connect with the California Overland Stages for Denver City, Sacramento, &c.

☞ Be sure and call for Tickets "*Via North Missouri Railway.*"

CARS WITH RUTTAN'S PATENT for Warming and Ventilating in Winter, and for Cooling and Ventilating in Summer, are in use on the *North Missouri Railway.*

☞ Tickets on sale at all the principal ticket offices in the country, and at No. 40 Fourth street, under "Planters' House," and the depot at North Market Street, St. Louis.

I. H. STURGEON,
Pres. & Gen. Supt.

H. H. WHEELER,
Gen. Ticket Agent.

ST. LOUIS TO ST. JOSEPH.		ST. JOSEPH TO ST. LOUIS.		
Exp	Mls	STATIONS.	Mls	Exp
A. M.		LEAVE — ARRIVE		P. M.
8 20	0	*St. Louis* [1]	305	8 32
	4	Bellefontaine	301	
	6	Jennings	299	
8 56	10	Ferguson	295	7 59
	12	Grahams	293	
9 11	14	Bridgton	291	7 46
9 32	19	Ferry Landing	286	7 25
10 16	20	*St. Charles* [2]	285	6 40
10 51	29	Dardenne	276	6 08
11 12	33	O'Fallon	272	5 55
11 25	37	Perruque	268	5 41
11 44	42	Wentzville	263	5 29
12 06	49	Millville	256	5 10
12 20	52	Wrights	253	4 58
1 12	58	*Warrenton* [3]	247	4 40
1 34	64	Pendleton	241	3 49
1 48	68	Jonesburg	237	3 33
2 05	73	High Hill	232	3 17
2 20	77	Florence	228	3 02
2 40	83	Montgomery	222	2 40
3 08	90	Wellsville	215	2 12
3 25	94	Martinsburg	211	1 53
3 48	101	Jeffstown	204	1 27
4 14	108	*Mexico*	197	1 01
5 05	121	Centralia	184	12 07
5 35	130	Sturgeon	175	11 37
6 11	140	Renick	165	10 58
6 36	147	Allen	158	10 32
7 15	158	Jacksonville	147	9 50
7 54	170	arrive } *Macon City* [4] { leave	135	9 10
8 30		leave } { arrive		8 50
9 05	174	Bevier	131	8 20
9 25	178	Callao	127	7 54
10 27	193	Bucklin	112	6 32
10 52	199	St. Catherine	106	6 28
11 40	203	*Brookfield*	102	6 10
12 05	208	Laclede	97	5 15
1 45	229	*Chillicothe* [5]	76	3 50
2 09	234	Utica	71	3 20
3 05	244	Breckenridge	61	2 20
3 47	255	Hamilton	50	1 36
5 15	270	Cameron	35	12 17
5 40	276	Osborn	29	11 48
6 17	284	Stewartsville	21	11 10
7 00	293	Easton	12	10 28
8 00	305	*St. Joseph* [6]	0	9 30
A. M.		ARRIVE — LEAVE		P. M.

☞ *No Sunday Trains.*

[1] Con. with Railways diverging from St. Louis. [2] Steamers to Nebraska, Kansas, &c. [3] Stages to all towns on the Missouri River. [4] Connects with Hannibal & St. Joseph Railway. [5] Stages to Brunswick. [6] Connects with Platte Co. Railway, and Steamers to Kansas City, Leavenworth, Council Bluffs, &c.

TROY & BOSTON AND WESTERN VERMONT RAILWAYS.

D. T. Vail, President; D. Robinson, Vice-President; C. W. Mosley, Supt. Troy, N. Y. F. C. White, Supt. Western Vermont Railway. L. A. McClure, Gen. Ticket Agent, Troy, N. Y. M. B. Waters, Passenger Agent, 273 Broadway, New York. [July 16.

GOING NORTH.						STATIONS.	GOING SOUTH.					
Mail	Exp. Fr't.	Exp.	Acc.	Nt. Exp.	Mls		Mls	Nt. Exp.	Acc.	Acc.	N.Y. Exp.	Mail
A. M.	M.	P. M.	P. M.	P. M.		LEAVE — ARRIVE		A. M.	P. M.	A. M.	P. M.	P. M.
8 15	12 00	1 00	4 45	9 45		*Troy* [1]	48	4 40	9 30	2 45	4 15	5 50
8 25	12 11	1 09	4 56	9 55	4	Lansingburgh	44	4 29	9 19	2 33	4 03	5 40
8 36	12 29	1 19	5 08	10 05	9	Akirs	39	4 18	9 10	2 22	3 52	5 30
8 41	12 42	1 25	5 16	10 13	12	Schaghticoke	35	4 10	9 02	2 13	3 43	5 23
8 47	12 47	1 28	5 20	10 16	14	Valley Falls	34	4 08	8 59	2 09	3 39	5 20
8 53	12 53	1 32	5 26	10 21	17	Johnsonville	31	4 03	8 53	2 02	3 32	5 15
9 04	1 13	1 42	5 39	10 32	21	Buskirks	27	3 54	8 40	1 50	3 20	5 04
9 09	1 25	1 45	5 45	10 35	23	Eagle Bridge [2]	25	3 50	8 36	1 45	3 15	4 58
9 15		1 50	5 50		26	Hoosick Junction	22		8 30	1 38		4 50
9 20		2 00	5 58		27	*Hoosick Falls*	21		8 16	1 30		4 45
9 27		2 09	6 06		30	Hoosick Corners	18		8 04	1 19		4 37
9 33		2 17	6 14		33	Petersburg	15		7 57	1 13		4 31
9 42		2 27	6 24		36	North Pownal	12		7 49	1 06		4 25
9 48		2 34	6 32		39	Pownal	9		7 41	1 00		4 19
9 57		2 44	6 43		43	Williamstown	5		7 32	12 52		4 11
10 02		2 50	6 49		45	Blackinton	3		7 27	12 46		4 06
10 10		3 00	6 55		48	*North Adams*			7 20	12 40		4 00
9 20		1 54	5 54		27	North Hoosick	57		8 24	1 35	11 40	4 41
9 24		1 58	5 58		28	Walloomsac	56		8 20	1 32	11 25	4 37
9 35		2 10	6 10		33	*North Bennington* [3]	52		8 12	1 25	11 00	4 25
9 41			6 17		35	South Shaftsbury	49		8 01		10 22	4 19
9 53			6 29		40	Shaftsbury	44		7 47		9 53	4 06
10 05			6 42		45	Arlington	39		7 35		9 16	3 54
10 12			6 50		48	Sunderland	36		7 27		8 55	3 46
10 30			7 05		54	*Manchester*	30		7 12		8 30	3 33
10 43			7 17		59	East Dorset	25		6 52		7 50	3 18
10 50			7 25		62	North Dorset	22		6 43		7 25	3 10
10 59			7 35		66	Danby	18		6 22		7 02	3 00
11 13			7 47		71	South Wallingford	13		6 19		6 32	2 48
11 22			7 58		75	Wallingford	9		6 09		6 09	2 39
11 30			8 05		78	Clarendon	6		6 00		5 46	2 30
11 45			8 20		84	*Rutland* [4]			5 45		5 27	2 15
A. M.	P. M.	P. M.	P. M.	P. M.		ARRIVE — LEAVE		A. M.	A. M.	P. M.	A. M.	P. M.

[1] Connects at Troy by Railway and Steamboat for New York; also, with Rensselaer & Saratoga and New York Central Railways.
[2] Connects with Rutland & Washington Railway.
[3] Branch Railway to Bennington, making close connections.
[4] Connects with Rutland & Burlington Railway for Burlington, Rouse's Point, Montreal, &c.

Through Routes from New York to Boston.—Via New York & New Haven; New Haven, Hartford & Springfield; Western; and Boston & Worcester Railways.

Leave New York at **8 00** A. M., 12 15, **3 00** & **8 00** P. M., arriving at Boston at **5 05** P. M., **12 15** & 6 00 A. M.

Returning—Leave Boston at **4 45** & **8 30** A. M., and **2 30** & **8 30** P. M.

Also by the following Steamboat Routes, leaving at 5 00 P. M., arr. at Boston about 6 00 A. M.

Via Steamboat to Fall River, and Old Colony & Boston Railway.

Via Steamboat to Stonington, and Boston & Providence Railway.

Via Steamboat to Norwich, and Norwich & Worcester and Boston & Worcester Railways.

ALBANY & SUSQUEHANNA RAILWAY.

Leave Albany for Unadilla, and way stations, at 7 30 A. M. and 1 10 P. M.
Returning—Leave Unadilla at 10 00 A. M. and 2 45 P. M. Distance 100 miles.

ALLEGHENY VALLEY RAILWAY.

Leave Pittsburg for Kittaning, Mahoning, and way stations, at 7 00 A. M. and 4 00 P. M.
Returning—Leave Mahoning at 6 20 A. M. and 2 15 P. M. Distance 44 miles.

ATLANTA & WEST POINT RAILWAY.

Leave Atlanta for West Point, and way stations, at 7 00 A. M.
Returning—Leave West Point at 11 45 P. M. Distance 87 miles.

ATLANTIC & GREAT WESTERN RAILWAY.

Leave Salamanca for Meadville, Warren, Cleveland, Cincinnati, and way stations, at 5 30 A. M. and **12 10**, 6 35 & **11 00** P. M.
Returning—Leave Cincinnati at 9 40 A. M. and **10 40** P. M., and Cleveland at 6 10 & **9 30** A. M., and 4 15 & **9 25** P. M. Distance to Cincinnati 418 miles.

Franklin Branch.—Leave Meadville for Franklin, Oil City, and way stations, at 6 15 A. M. and 2 30 P. M.
Returning—Leave Oil City at 9 15 A. M. and 2 30 P. M. Distance 36 miles.

ATLANTIC & NORTH CAROLINA RAILWAY.

Leave Goldsboro for Newburn, Morehead City, and way stations, at 8 15 A. M.
Returning at 3 15 P. M. Distance 95 miles.

BALTIMORE & OHIO RAILWAY.

Leave Baltimore for Harper's Ferry, Grafton, Wheeling, and way stations, at 8 50 A. M. and 9 00 P. M.
Returning—Leave Wheeling at 7 00 A. M. and 12 28 & 8 25 P. M. Distance 379 miles.

Washington Branch.—Leave Baltimore for Washington, and way stations, at 4 10, 7 05, 8 45 & 9 45 A. M., and 3 15, 4 15 & 7 45 P. M.
Returning—Leave Washington at 7 00, 8 00 & 11 15 A. M., and 2 45, 4 30, 6 30 & 7 30 P. M. Distance 40 miles.

BELLEFONTAINE RAILWAY.

Leave Cleveland for Bellefontaine, Indianapolis, and way stations, at 7 45 A. M. and **8 20** P. M.
Returning—Leave Indianapolis at **4 00** A. M. and 7 45 P. M. Distance 282 miles.

BELVIDERE, DELAWARE & FLEMINGTON RAILWAY.

Leave Philadelphia for Manunka Chunk, Scranton, Great Bend, and way stations, at 7 30 A. M and 3 30 P. M.
Returning—Leave Great Bend at 7 30 A. M. and 2 00 P. M. Distance 213 miles.

BOSTON & MAINE RAILWAY.

Leave Boston for Portland, and way stations, at 7 00, **7 30** & 10 15 A. M. and 12 00 M., and **3 00** 5 00 & 6 00 P. M.
Returning—Leave Portland at 8 40 A. M. and 2 50 P. M. Distance 111 miles.

BOSTON & WORCESTER RAILWAY.

Leave Boston for Worcester, and way stations, and 7 00 A. M. and 1 30 & 4 30 P. M. Express Trains leave for Framingham and Worcester only, at **4 45** & **8 30 A. M.**, and **2 30, 5 30** & **8 30** P. M.
Returning—Leave Worcester at **4 15**, 6 50, **9 25** & 9 45 A. M., and 2 00, **3 40**, 4 15, **10 50** & **12 00** P. M. Extra Trains for Lower Falls and Brookline. Distance 45 miles.

BOSTON & LOWELL RAILWAY.

Leave Boston for Lowell and Wilton at 7 00, **8 00**, 10 00 A. M. & **12 00** M., and 2 30, **5 30** & 6 00 P. M.
Returning—Leave Lowell at 7 00, 7 30 & **9 34** A. M., and **12 20**, 2 15, **5 30** & **9 30** P. M. Leave Wilton, at 6 15 & **11 00** A. M., and 3 30 P. M. Distance 55 miles.

BOSTON & PROVIDENCE RAILWAY.

Leave Boston for Providence at 7 25, 10 30 & **11 10** A. M., and 4 00, **5 30** & **8 30** P. M.
Returning—Leave Providence at **4 20**, 7 00 & 10 40 A. M., and 4 10 & **7 30** P. M.
Connecting with cars for Stonington and New London, and with steamboat to and from New York daily. Distance 43 miles.

BURLINGTON & MISSOURI RAILWAY.

Leave Burlington for Ottumwa, and way stations, at 5 00 A. M. and **2** 40 P. M.
Returning—Leave Ottumwa at 10 00 A. M. and 7 45 P. M. Distance 115 miles.

CAMDEN & AMBOY RAILWAY.

VIA STEAMBOAT AND RAILWAY.

Leave Pier No. 1, New York, for Bordentown, Camden, Philadelphia, and way stations, at 5 00 A. M. and **2 00** & 4 00 P. M.
Returning—Leave Philadelphia at 5 00 A. M. and **2 00** & 5 30 P. M. Distance 92 Miles.

CAMDEN & ATLANTIC RAILWAY.

Leave Philadelphia for Camden, Waterford, Atlantic, and way stations, at 7 30 A. M. and 2 00 P. M.
Returning—Leave Atlantic at 7 08 A. M. and 4 42 P. M. Distance 60 miles.

CATAWISSA RAILWAY.

Leave Philadelphia for Catawissa, Williamsport, and way stations, at 8 15 A. M. and 3 30 P. M.
Returning—Leave Williamsport at 8 45 A. M. and 1 32 P. M. Distance 197 miles.

CENTRAL RAILWAY OF NEW JERSEY.

Leave New York for Elizabeth, Easton, and way stations, at **7 00**, 8 00 & **9 00** A. M., 12 00 M., and 4 00, 5 00, 6 15, 7 30 & **8 00** P. M.
Returning—Leave Easton at **2 10**, **7 09** & 7 20 A. M., and **1 10**, 1 35 & **7 20** P. M. Extra Trains from New York, to way stations. Distance 75 miles.

CENTRAL OHIO RAILWAY.

Leave Columbus for Newark, Zanesville, Bellaire, and way stations, at 5 00 A. M. and 2 35 P. M.
Returning—Leave Bellaire at 5 00 A. M. and 3 50 P. M. Distance 137 miles.

CHESHIRE RAILWAY.

Leave Fitchburg for Keene, Bellows Falls, and way stations, at 9 15 A. M. and 1 25 & **7 25** P. M.
Returning—Leave Bellows Falls at **3 50** & 8 00 A. M., and 2 40 P. M. Distance 64 miles.

CHICAGO, BURLINGTON & QUINCY RAILWAY.

Leave Chicago for Galesburg, Burlington, Quincy, and way stations, at 8 20 A. M. and 4 30 P. M. & 12 00 night.
Returning—Leave Quincy at 3 15 A. M. and 4 00 P. M., and Burlington at 6 00 A. M. and 7 00 P. M. Distance to Quincy 265 miles.

CHICAGO, ALTON & ST. LOUIS RAILWAY.

Leave Chicago for Joliet, Bloomington, Springfield, Alton, St. Louis, and way stations, at 8 10 A. M. and 4 45 & **8 05** P. M.
Returning—Leave St. Louis at 7 30 A. M. and 3 50 P. M. Distance 280 miles.

CHICAGO & GREAT EASTERN RAILWAY.

Leave Chicago for Logansport, Cincinnati, and way stations, at 6 00 A. M. and 5 30 & 9 00 P. M.
Returning leave Cincinnati at 7 00 A. M. and 5 40 P. M. Distance 294 miles.

CHICAGO, MILWAUKEE, LA CROSSE & ST. PAUL RAILWAY.

Leave Chicago for Waukegan, Kenosha, Racine, Milwaukee, La Crosse, and way stations, at 9 00 A. M., and 2 00, 4 20 & 5 04 P. M.
Returning—Leave La Crosse at 5 00 A. M. and 1 00 P. M. Distance 280 miles.

CHICAGO & NORTH WESTERN RAILWAY.

Wisconsin Division.—Leave Chicago for Janesville, Fond du Lac, Oshkosh, Fort Howard and way stations, at 9 00 A. M., and 4 30 P. M.
Returning—Leave Fort Howard at 6 30 A. M., and 3 15 P. M. Distance 242 miles.

Galena Division.—Leave Chicago for Elgin, Rockford, Freeport, Dunleith, and way stations, at 9 00 A. M., and 10 00 P. M.
Returning—Leave Dunleith at 5 15 A. M., and 4 00 P. M. Distance 188 miles.

Dixon & Iowa Division.—Leave Chicago for De Kalb, Dixon, Cedar Rapids, Boonsboro, and way stations, at 8 15 A. M. and 7 00 P. M.
Returning—Leave Boonsboro at 10 00 A. M., and Cedar Rapids at 6 45 A. M., and 5 20 P. M. Distance 342 miles.

Beloit & Madison Branch.—Leave Chicago for Beloit, Madison and way stations, at 4 30 P. M.
Returning—Leave Madison at 7 50 A. M. and 3 15 P. M. Distance 138 miles.

CHICAGO & ROCK ISLAND RAILWAY.

Leave Chicago for Joliet, Peoria, Rock Island, Davenport, and way stations, at 9 00 A. M., 4 45 P. M. and 12 00 night.
Returning—Leave Davenport at 7 35 A. M. and 7 50 P. M. Distance 184 miles.

CINCINNATI, HAM. & DAYTON, and DAY. & MICH. RAILWAYS.

Leave Cincinnati for Dayton, Toledo, Detroit, and way stations, at 7 00 & 9 40 A. M., and 3 00, 5 40, 6 00 & **10 50** P. M. For Hamilton only at 7 00 P. M.
Returning—Leave Dayton for Cincinnati at 3 50 & 7 20 A. M., and 3 00, 4 10 & 6 40 P. M. Accommodation Trains from Hamilton at 4 00, 6 40 & 9 50 A. M. Distance 267 miles.

CINCINNATI & ZANESVILLE RAILWAY.

Leave Cincinnati for Zanesville, and way stations, at 8 25 A. M. and 4 00 P. M.
Returning—Leave Zanesville at 9 55 A. M. and 1 00 P. M. Distance 168 miles.

CLEVELAND, COLUMBUS & CINCINNATI RAILWAY.

Leave Cleveland for Crestline, Columbus, and way stations, at **6 30** A. M. and 2 45 & **8 20** P. M.
Returning—Leave Columbus at **11 10** & **12 45** A. M., and 3 00 P. M. Distance 138 miles.

CLEVELAND & PITTSBURG RAILWAY.

Leave Cleveland for Alliance, Wellsville, Pittsburg and way stations, at 8 10 A. M., and **2 40** & 3 40 P. M.
Returning—Leave Pittsburg at 6 10 A. M., and 3 30 & **1 55** P. M. Distance 150 miles.

River Division.—Leave Pittsburg for Wheeling at 6 10 A. M., and 1 55 & 4 35 P. M.
Returning—Leave Belle Air at 6 10 & 10 40 A. M., and 4 05 P. M. Distance 95 miles.

CLEVELAND & TOLEDO RAILWAY.

Leave Cleveland for Grafton, Fremont, and Toledo, at **8 30** A. M. and 2 40 & **6 25** P. M., and for Sandusky at 4 00 P. M.
Returning—Leave Toledo, at **4 50** & 9 55 A. M., and **5 05** P. M., and leaving Sandusky at 6 45 A. M. Distance 113 miles.

COLUMBUS & INDIANAPOLIS RAILWAY.

Leave Columbus for Urbana, Piqua, Richmond, Indianapolis, and way stations, at 9 20 A. M. and 1 00. 5 00 & **11 45** P. M.
Returning—Leave Indianapolis at **4 15** A. M. and 2 45 & **8 00** P. M. Distance 188 miles.

CONCORD, MANCHESTER & LAWRENCE RAILWAY.

Leave Boston for Lowell, Nashua, Manchester, and Concord, at 7 00 & **8 00** A. M. and 12 00 M., and 2 30 & 5 30 P. M.
Returning—Leave Concord at 5 30, 7 30 & 10 15 A. M., and 3 30 & 7 45 P. M.
Leave Boston via Lawrence for Concord, at 7 30 instead of 8 00 A. M. as above. All other trains same as above.

CONNECTICUT & PASSUMPSIC RAILWAY.

Leave Newport for St. Johnsbury, Wells River, White River Junction, and way stations, at 7 15 A. M. and 7 00 P. M.
Returning—Leave White River Junction, at 8 20 A. M. and 1 45 P. M. Distance 105 miles.

CONNECTICUT RIVER RAILWAY.

Leave Springfield for Northampton, Greenfield, South Vernon, and way stations, at 7 45 A. M. and 2 00 & 6 30 P. M.
Returning—Leave South Vernon at 4 35 & 9 23 A. M., and 3 40 P. M. Distance 50 miles.

CUMBERLAND VALLEY RAILWAY.

Leave Harrisburg for Carlisle, Chambersburg, Hagerstown, and way stations, at 8 40 A. M. and 2 00 P. M.
Returning—Leave Hagerstown at 8 10 A. M. and 12 00 M. Distance 74 miles.

DANBURY & NORWALK RAILWAY.

Leave Danbury for South Norwalk, at 6 25 A. M. and 12 10 & 4 55 P. M.
Returning—Leave South Norwalk for Danbury, at 9 00 A. M., and 2 00 & 6 35 P. M. Distance 24 miles.

DAYTON & UNION RAILWAY.

Leave Dayton for Union City, and way stations, at 10 15 A. M. and 1 50 P. M.
Returning—Leave Union City at 7 30 A. M. and 2 40 P. M. Distance 47 miles.

DELAWARE & HUDSON RAILWAY.

Leave Scranton for Providence, Carbondale, and way stations, at 10 20 A. M. and 4 20 P. M.
Returning—Leave Carbondale for Scranton, at 8 20 A. M. and 2 20 P. M. Distance 17 miles.

DELAWARE RAILWAY.

Leave Wilmington for Salisbury, and way stations, at 10 35 A. M., and for Harrington, 6 00 P. M.
Returning—Leave Salisbury for Wilmington, at 10 30 A. M., and Harrington at 6 10 A. M. and 12 30 P. M. Distance 103 miles.

DELAWARE, LACKAWANNA & WESTERN RAILWAY.

Leave New York for Manunka Chunk, Scranton, Great Bend, and way stations, at 9 00 A. M. and 4 00 P. M.
Returning—Leave Great Bend at 1 50 & 7 15 P. M. Distance 190 miles.

DETROIT & MILWAUKEE RAILWAY.

Leave Detroit for Owasso, Grand Haven, Milwaukee, and way stations, at 8 00 & 10 30 A. M., and 8 00 P. M.
Returning—Leave Milwaukee at 8 00 P. M. Distance 274 miles.

DOVER & WINNIPISSEOGEE RAILWAY.

Leave Dover for Alton Bay, and way stations, at 11 00 A. M. and 5 50 P. M.
Returning—Leave Alton Bay at 8 30 A. M. and 2 45 P. M. Distance 28 miles.

DUBUQUE & SIOUX CITY RAILWAY.

Leave Dubuque for Cedar Rapids, Cedar Falls, and way stations, at 10 00 A. M.
Returning—Leave Cedar Falls at 8 50 A. M. Not completed.

EASTERN (MASS.) RAILWAY.

Leave Boston for Lynn, Salem, Newburyport, Portsmouth, Portland, and way stations, at 7 15, **7 30** & 10 30 A. M., and 12 15, **3 00**, 5 00 & 6 10 P. M.
Returning—Leave Portsmouth at 6 15, 9 00 & **11 15** A. M., and **5 30** P. M., and Portland at **8 40** A. M. and **2 50** P. M. Distance 108 miles.

EAST PENNSYLVANIA RAILWAY.

Leave Reading for Lyons, Allentown, and way stations, **4 49** & **10 52** A. M., and 4 25 P. M.
Returning—Leave Allentown at 7 00 A. M., and 4 15 & **12 35** P. M. Distance 36 miles.

EAST TENNESSEE & GEORGIA RAILWAY.

Leave Knoxville for Athens, Chattanooga, and way stations, at 7 10 A. M. and 8 30 P. M.
Returning—Leave Chattanooga at 7 00 A. M. and 7 25 P. M. Distance 112 miles.

EAST TENNESSEE & VIRGINIA RAILWAY.

Leave Bristol for Russellville, Knoxville, and way stations, at 12 20 A. M.
Returning—Leave Knoxville at 12 30 P. M. Distance 130 miles.

ERIE RAILWAY.

Leave New York for Dunkirk, Buffalo, and way stations, at **7 45** & 10 00 A. M., and 3 00, 4 30, **5 30**, **7 00** & **8 00** P. M.
Returning—Leave Dunkirk at 7 10 & 9 30 A. M., and **4 15** P. M. Leave Buffalo at **5 30** & 8 30 A. M., and **2 20**, **6 15** & **10 45** P. M. Distance to Buffalo 423 miles.

EVANSVILLE & CRAWFORDSVILLE RAILWAY.

Leave Evansville for Vincennes, Terre Haute and Rockville, at 5 40 & 9 15 A. M. and 2 20 P. M.
Returning—Leave Rockville at 9 30 A. M., Terre Haute at 6 50 A. M., and 3 40 P. M. Distance 109 miles.

FITCHBURG & BOSTON RAILWAY.

Leave Boston for Fitchburg, and way stations, at 6 20, **7 30** & 11 00 A. M., and 2 15, 4 00, **5 30**, 6 00 & 7 30 P. M.
Returning—Leave Fitchburg at **6 40** & 7 20 A. M., and 12 15 & 5 15 P. M. Distance 50 miles.

GEORGIA RAILWAY.

Leave Augusta for Atlanta, and way stations, at 7 00 A. M. and 5 30 P. M.
Returning—Leave Atlanta at 7 05 A. M. and 6 30 P. M. Distance 171 miles.

GRAND TRUNK RAILWAY.

Going West—Leave Portland for Quebec, Montreal, Toronto, Detroit, and way stations, at 7 00 A. M. and 1 10 P. M.; Montreal at 7 00 & 9 05 A. M. and 9 00 P. M.; Toronto at **1 00** & 7 30 A. M. and 3 45 P. M.; Quebec at 7 00 A. M. and 2 00 & 7 40 P. M.

BUFFALO DIVISION.—Leave Buffalo for Brantford, Goderich, Detroit, and way stations, at **12 30** & 7 00 A. M., and **1 25** & 3 30 P. M.

Going East—Leave Detroit at 6 15 & **10 00** A. M. and 6 00 P. M.; Toronto at 6 30 A. M., and 12 30 & 6 00 P. M.; Montreal at 7 00 A. M., and 2 00 & **10 10** P. M.

GREAT WESTERN RAILWAY.

Leave Suspension Bridge for Hamilton, Toronto, Paris, London, Bothwell, (oil regions,) Detroit, and way stations, at 7 00 A. M., and **1 30**, 3 35 & **12 15** P. M. (Lightning Express.)
Returning—Leave Detroit at **6 30** A. M., and 10 00 & **7 00** P. M. Distance 230 miles.

GREENVILLE & COLUMBIA RAILWAY.

Leave Columbia for Abbeville, Anderson, Greenville, and way stations, at 7 00 A. M.
Returning—Leave Greenville at 5 55 A. M. Distance 143 miles.

HANNIBAL & ST. JOSEPH RAILWAY.

Leave Hannibal for Macon City, St. Joseph, and way stations, at 7 30 A. M. and 3 00 P. M.
Returning—Leave St. Joseph at 4 30 A. M. and 11 00 P. M. Distance 206 miles.

HOUSATONIC RAILWAY.

Leave Bridgeport for Pittsfield, at 10 30 A. M.; for New Milford, at 5 45 P. M.
Returning—Leave Pittsfield for Bridgeport, at 8 45 A. M.; for Barrington, at 5 00 P. M. Distance 110 miles.

HUDSON RIVER RAILWAY.

Leave New York for Poughkeepsie, Albany, Troy, and way stations, at 6 40, **7 45** & **10 00** A. M., and **4 00**, 5 15, **7 00** & **11 00** P. M.
Returning—Leave Troy at 4 50 & 9 50 A. M., and **4 40** & **10 45** P. M.; Albany at **1 45**, **5 15** & **10 15** A. M., and **4 40** & **10 45** P. M. Distance 150 miles.

ILLINOIS CENTRAL RAILWAY.

Leave Dunleith for Freeport, Dixon, Bloomington, Centralia, Cairo, and way stations, at 6 00 A. M. and 5 00 P. M.
Returning—Leave Cairo at 2 30 A. M. and 12 30 P. M. Distance 456 miles.

CHICAGO BRANCH.—Leave Chicago for Centralia, Cairo, and way stations, at 9 00 A. M. and 10 05 P. M.
Returning—Leave Cairo at 2 30 A. M. and 12 30 P. M. Distance 365 miles.

INDIANAPOLIS, PERU & CHICAGO RAILWAY.

Leave Indianapolis for Peru, and way stations, at 12 30 & 10 10 P. M.
Returning—Leave Peru at 3 00 A. M. and 12 25 P. M. Distance 75 miles.

INDIANAPOLIS & CINCINNATI RAILWAY.

Leave Cincinnati for Lawrenceburg, Shelbyville, Indianapolis, and way stations, at 7 10 A. M., and 1 20, 4 30 & **5 00** P. M.
Returning—Leave Indianapolis at 4 00 & 11 00 A. M., and 7 25 P. M. Distance 115 miles.

INDIANAPOLIS & MADISON RAILWAY.

Leave Madison for Columbus, Indianapolis, and way stations, at 6 00 A. M. and 2 35 P. M.
Returning—Leave Indianapolis at 3 00 P. M. Distance 86 miles.

JEFFERSONVILLE RAILWAY.

Leave Louisville for Indianapolis, and way stations, at 6 30 A. M., and 1 45 & **8 30** P. M.
Returning—Leave Indianapolis at 10 15 A. M., and 5 00 & **9 00** P. M. Distance 108 miles.

KENTUCKY CENTRAL RAILWAY.

Leave Covington for Cynthiana, Lexington, and way stations, at 6 00 A. M. and 1 50 P. M.
Returning—Leave Lexington at 5 50 A. M. and 1 00 P. M. Distance 99 miles.

LACKAWANNA & BLOOMSBURG RAILWAY.

Leave Scranton for Lackawanna, Kingston, Northumberland, and way stations, at 5 50 A. M. and 4 40 P. M.
Returning—Leave Northumberland at 7 00 A. M. and 5 20 P. M. Distance 80 miles.

LAYFAYETTE & INDIANAPOLIS RAILWAY.

Leave Indianapolis for Layfayette, and way stations, at 12 40, 7 30 & 9 10 P. M.
Returning—Leave Lafayette at 1 10 & 6 50 A. M., and 1 15 P. M. Distance 64 miles.

LEHIGH VALLEY RAILWAY.

Leave Easton for Mauch Chunk, White Haven, and way stations, at 9 47 A. M., and 3 25 & 7 40 P. M.
Returning—Leave White Haven at 9 30 A. M. and 3 00 P. M.; Mauch Chunk at 4 30 & 10 47 A. M., and 4 25 P. M. Distance 71 miles.

LITTLE MIAMI & COLUMBUS & XENIA RAILWAY.

Leave Cincinnati for Xenia, Columbus, and way stations, at **6 00** & **8 25** A. M., and 4 00, 5 45, **8 00** & **11 40** P. M.
Returning—Leave Columbus at **2 00**, 7 20 & **11 30** A. M., and **11 00** P. M. Distance 120 miles.

LONG ISLAND RAILWAY.

Leave New York for Greenport, and way stations, at 8 00 A. M. and 3 30 P. M.
Leave New York for Hempstead, at 8 00 & 10 30 A. M., and 3 30 & 4 30 P. M. Distance 99 miles.

LOUISVILLE, FRANKFORT & LEXINGTON RAILWAY.

Leave Louisville for Frankfort, Lexington, and way stations, at 6 00 A. M., and 2 20 & 5 15 P. M.
Returning—Leave Lexington at 5 35 A. M. and **2 00** P. M. Distance 112 miles.

LOUISVILLE, NEW ALBANY & CHICAGO RAILWAY.

Leave New Albany for Bloomington, Lafayette, Michigan City, Chicago, and way stations, at 9 30 A. M. and 9 20 P. M.
Returning—Leave Michigan City, at 8 30 A. M. and 8 45 P. M. Distance 288 miles.

LOUISVILLE, NASHVILLE, CLARKSVILLE & MEMP. RAILWAY.

(See Advertisement. Page 80.)

Leave Louisville for Mumfordsville, Bowling Green, Nashville, and way stations, at 7 00 A. M. and 7 00 P. M.
Returning—Leave Nashville at 7 45 A. M. and 6 30 P. M. Distance 185 miles.

MACON & WESTERN RAILWAY.

Leave Atlanta for Macon, and way stations, at 8 00 A. M. and 7 10 P. M.
Returning—Leave Macon at 8 00 A. M. and 7 00 P. M. Distance 103 miles.

MAINE CENTRAL RAILWAY.

Leave Portland for Bangor, and way stations, at 7 00 A. M. and 1 10 P. M.
Returning—Leave Bangor at 7 30 A. M. and 2 15 P. M. Distance 138 miles.

MARIETTA & CINCINNATI RAILWAY.

Leave Cincinnati for Chillicothe, Marietta, Belpre, and way stations, at 12 35 & 9 00 A. M., and 4 00 P. M.
Returning—Leave Belpre at 6 35 A. M. and 7 00 P. M. Distance 205 miles.

MEMPHIS & CHARLESTON RAILWAY.

Leave Memphis for Corinth, Decatur, Stevenson, Chattanooga, and way stations, at 6 25 A. M.
Returning—Leave Stevenson at 12 15 P. M. Distance 272 miles.

MICHIGAN CENTRAL RAILWAY.

Leave Detroit for Jackson, Kalamazoo, Chicago, and way stations, at 6 15 & 10 30 A. M., and **5 25**, **11 00** & 4 15 P. M.
Returning—Leave Chicago at 4 00 & **6 00** A. M., and **5 30**, 5 45 & 10 00 P. M. Distance 281 miles.

MICHIGAN SOUTHERN & NORTHERN INDIANA RAILWAY.

Leave Toledo for Chicago, via Bryan, Goshen, and way stations, at 1 10 A. M. and **12 45** P. M., and via Adrian, White Pigeon, and way stations, at 7 50 A. M. and **7 40** P. M.
Returning—Leave Chicago, via Bryan, &c., at **7 00** A. M. and 5 30 P. M., and via Adrian, at 6 00 A. M. and **10 00** P. M. Distance 244 miles.

MILWAUKEE & PRAIRIE DU CHIEN RAILWAY.

Leave Milwaukee for Waukesha, Madison, Prairie du Chien, and way stations, at 11 10 A. M. and 6 00 P. M., connecting with River Steamers.
Returning—Leave Prairie du Chien at 7 20 A. M. and 4 00 P. M. Distance 194 miles.

MILWAUKEE & ST. PAUL RAILWAY.

Leave Milwaukee for Watertown, Portage City, La Crosse, and way stations, at 1 40 & 8 50 P. M., connecting with River Steamers.
Returning—Leave La Crosse at 6 00 A. M. and 6 15 P. M. Distance 195 miles.

MINNESOTA CENTRAL RAILWAY.

Leave Minneapolis for Faribault, and way stations, at 8 45 A. M. and 3 40 P. M.
Returning—Leave Faribault at 6 00 A. M. and 1 40 P. M. Distance 56 miles.

MISSISSIPPI & TENNESSEE RAILWAY.

Leave Memphis for Grenada, and way stations, at 4 30 P. M.
Returning—Leave Grenada at 2 30 A. M. Distance 99 miles.

MOBILE & OHIO RAILWAY.

Leave Mobile for Meridian, Columbus, (Miss.) Corinth, Jackson, Columbus, (Ky.) Cairo, and way stations, at 2 00 P. M.
Returning—Leave Columbus at 7 00 A. M. Distance 472 miles.

MONTREAL & CHAMPLAIN RAILWAY.

Leave Montreal for Rouse's Point, and way stations, at 5 30 A. M. and 3 30 P. M., and for St. Johns 8 30 A. M.
Returning—Leave Rouse's Point 7 00 A. M. and **9 00** P. M., and St. Johns at 8 00 A. M. and 7 50 & **9 50** P. M. Distance 44 miles.

MORRIS & ESSEX RAILWAY.

Leave New York for Hackettstown, and way stations, at 8 30 & 11 30 A. M., and **4 10**, 5 00 & 6 30 P. M.
Returning—Leave Hackettstown at **6 45** A. M. and 1 45 P. M. Distance 62 miles.

NASHVILLE & CHATTANOOGA RAILWAY.

Leave Nashville for Murfreesboro, Chattanooga, and way stations, at 7 40 A. M. and 4 35 P. M.
Returning—Leave Chattanooga at 6 15 A. M. and 9 20 P. M. Distance 151 miles.

NASHVILLE & DECATUR RAILWAY.

Leave Nashville for Columbia, Athens, Decatur, and way stations, at 9 50 A. M. and 8 30 P. M.
Returning—Leave Decatur at 6 20 A. M. and 8 00 P. M. Distance 122 miles.

NAUGATUCK RAILWAY.

Leave Bridgeport for Waterbury, Winsted, and way stations, at 10 15 A. M., and 130 & 5 20 P. M.
Returning—Leave Winsted at 6 40 A. M. and 2 10 P. M. Distance 62 miles.

NEW LONDON, AMHERST & BELCHERTOWN RAILWAY.

Leave New London for Palmer, Amherst, and way stations, at 7 35 A. M. and 1 45 P. M.
Returning—Leave Amherst at 6 15 A. M. and 4 00 P. M., and Palmer at 7 50 A. M. and 2 15 P. M. Distance 86 miles.

NEW HAVEN & NORTHAMPTON RAILWAY.

Leave New Haven for Granby, Northampton, and way stations, at 5 15 A. M. and 3 20 P. M.
Returning—Leave Northampton at 6 15 and 10 50 A. M. Distance 76 miles.

NEW HAVEN, HARTFORD & SPRINGFIELD RAILWAY.

Leave Springfield for Hartford, New Haven, and way stations, at 7 00 A. M. & **12 00** M., and 2 20, **6 00**, 8 20 & **12 00** P. M.
Returning—Leave New Haven at 8 10 & **10 55** A. M., and 3 15, **6 05**, 8 05, & **11 15** P. M. Distance 62 miles.

NORTH EASTERN (S. C.) RAILWAY.

Leave Charleston for Florence, and way stations, at 12 00 M.
Returning—Leave Florence at 4 30 A. M. Distance 102 miles.

NEW ORLEANS, JACKSON & MISSISSIPPI CENT. RAILWAY.

Leave, New Orleans for Jackson, Grand Junction, Jackson, (Tenn.) Columbus, and Cairo, at 7 00 A. M.
Returning—Leave Grand Junction at 7 50 P. M. Distance 519 miles.

NEW JERSEY RAILWAY.

Leave Cortland St., New York, for New Brunswick, Trenton, Philadelphia, Baltimore, and Washington, at 7 00, **8 00** & **10 00** A. M. and **12 00** M., and **4 00**, 6 00, **7 00** & **12 00** P. M.
Returning—Leave Philadelphia at **8 00** A. M., and leave Washington at **7 30** & **11 15** A. M., and **4 35** & **6 30** P. M.

NEW YORK & HARLEM RAILWAY.

Leave New York for Chatham Corners and Troy, at 8 15, 10 00 & **11 00** A. M., and 2 30, 4 00, **5 00** & 5 10 P. M. Extra way Trains to and from White Plains.
Returning—Leave Troy at 6 10 A. M. and 3 10 P. M. Distance 160 miles.

NEW YORK & NEW HAVEN RAILWAY.

Leave New York for New Haven, Bridgeport, and way stations, at 7 00, **8 00**, 9 30, & 11 30 A. M., and **12 15**, **3 00**, 3 45, 4 30, 5 30, 6 30 & **8 00** P. M.
Returning—Leave New Haven at **2 15**, 5 30, **6 30**, **9 45** & 10 00 A. M., and **2 05**, **4 30**, 5 00 & **8 00** P. M. Distance 76 miles.

NORTHERN (CANADA) RAILWAY.

Leaves Toronto for Collingwood, and way stations, at 7 00 A. M. and 4 00 P. M.
Returning—Leaves Collingwood at 5 30 A. M. and 3 30 P. M. Distance 94 miles.

NORTHERN (N. H.) RAILWAY.

Leave Concord for West Lebanon, and way stations, at **10 40** & **10 35** A. M., and 3 21 & 8 35 P. M.
Returning—Leave West Lebanon at 1 20 A. M., and 12 20 & 5 20 P. M.

NORWICH & WORCESTER RAILWAY.

Leave Worcester for Norwich, connecting with steamboat for New York daily, at 6 30 & 10 30 A. M., and 4 00 & **7 00** P. M.
Returning—Leave Norwich at **1 15**, 6 00 & 11 30 A. M., and 8 30 P. M. Distance 73 miles.

OGDENSBURG & LAKE CHAMPLAIN RAILWAY.

Leave Ogdensburg for Malone, Rouse's Point, and way stations, at 5 30 A. M. and 11 30 P. M.
Returning—Leave Rouse's Point at 7 15 A. M. and 7 30 P. M. Distance 118 miles.

OIL CREEK RAILWAY.

Leave Corry for Titusville, Shaffer, and way stations, at 9 15 A. M. and 4 00 P. M.
Returning—Leave Shaffer at 5 15 A. M. and 12 00 M. Distance 34 miles.

OHIO & MISSISSIPPI RAILWAY.

Leave Cincinnati for North Vernon, Vincennes, Sandoval, St. Louis, and way stations, at 7 00 A. M. and **7 15** & **3 45** P. M.
Returning—Leave St. Louis at 6 00 A. M. and **4 00** & 6 00 P. M. Distance 340 miles.

OLD COLONY & NEWPORT RAILWAY.

Leave Boston for Fall River, and Newport, at **8 00** & 11 30 A. M., and 3 30, **4 30**, **5 30** & 6 00 P. M., connecting with steamboat for New York.
Returning—Leave Newport at **4 00**, 6 15 & **8 00** A. M., and 3 00 & 4 00 P. M. Distance 54 miles.

ORANGE & ALEXANDRIA RAILWAY.

Leave Washington for Gordonsville, Linchburg, and way stations, at 6 25 A. M.
Returning—Leave Lynchburg at 7 10 A. M. Distance 178 miles.

OTTAWA & PRESCOTT RAILWAY.

Leave Prescott for Ottawa, and way stations, at 2 20 & 6 00 P. M.
Returning—Leave Ottawa at 7 00 A. M. and 6 30 P. M. Distance 54 miles.

PACIFIC RAILWAY.

Leave St. Louis for Jefferson City, Kansas City, and way stations, at **7 45** A. M. and 4 10 & 5 45 P. M.
Returning—Leave Kansas City at 12 40 A. M. Distance 283 miles.

PENNSYLVANIA CENTRAL RAILWAY.

Leave Philadelphia for Harrisburg, Altoona, Pittsburg, and way stations, at 7 50, **9 50**, & **11 50** A. M., and 2 20, 3 50, 8 50 & **11 00** P. M.
Returning—Leave Pittsburg at **3 10**, 8 00 & **10 00** A. M., and 3 00, **4 20** & **10 10** P. M. Distance 355 miles.

PHILADELPHIA & ERIE RAILWAY.

Leave Philadelphia for Harrisburg, Erie, and way stations, at 7 50 & **11 50** A. M., and 8 50 P. M.
Returning—Leave Erie at **10 25** A. M., and 4 45 & 7 00 P. M. Distance 451 miles.

PHILADELPHIA & READING RAILWAY.

Leave Philadelphia for Reading, Pottsville, and way stations, at **8 15** A. M. and **3 30** & 5 00 P. M., and for Harrisburg via Reading, at 8 15 A. M. and 3 30 P. M.
Returning—Leave Pottsville for Philadelphia, at 8 45 A. M. and 1 00 & 2 45 P. M., and leaving Harrisburgh at 3 00 & 8 10 A. M. and 2 10 P. M.

PHILADELPHIA, WILMINGTON & BALTIMORE RAILWAY.

Leave Philadelphia for Wilmington, Havre de Grace, and Baltimore, at **4 15**, 8 15, 9 00, 11 15 & **11 45** A. M., and **3 00** & **11 00** P. M.
Returning—Leave Baltimore at 7 25 & **9 20** A. M., and **1 10**, **6 35** & **8 25** P. M. Distance 98 miles.

PITTSBURG & CONNELLSVILLE RAILWAY.

Leave Pittsburg for Uniontown, and way stations, at 7 00 A. M. and 3 00 P. M.
Returning—Leave Uniontown for Pittsburg, and way stations, at 5 30 A. M. and 1 15 P. M. Distance 72 miles.

PITTSBURG, FT. WAYNE & CHICAGO RAILWAY.

Leave Pittsburg for Alliance, Mansfield, Crestline, Ft. Wayne and Chicago at **2 05**, A. M. and 2 10 & 11 00 P. M.
Returning—Leave Chicago at **7 00** A. M., and 5 30 & 10 00 P. M. Distance 468 miles.

PITTSBURG, COLUMBUS & CINCINNATI RAILWAY.

Leave Pittsburg for Steubenville, Newark, Columbus, and way stations, at 4 15 A. M. and 12 58 & **4 25** P. M.
Returning—Leave Columbus at 5 00 A. M. and **2 35** & **11 40** P. M. Distance 193 miles.

PITTSBURG & ERIE RAILWAY.

Leave New Castle for Erie at 9 10 A. M.
Returning—Leave Erie at 10 50 A. M. Distance 148 miles.

PLATTSBURG & MONTREAL RAILWAY.

Leave Plattsburg for Montreal, and way stations, at 6 00 A. M. and 3 00 P. M.
Returning—Leave Montreal at 3 00 P. M. Distance 63 miles.

PORTLAND & KENNEBEC RAILWAY.

Leave Portland for Gardiner, Augusta, Skowhegan, and way stations, at 1 00 & 3 45 P. M.
Returning—Leave Skowhegan at 9 00 A. M. and 2 30 P. M. Distance 100 miles.

PROVIDENCE & WORCESTER RAILWAY.

Leave Worcester for Woonsocket, Providence, and way stations, at 7 00 & 11 30 A. M., and 4 00 P. M.
Returning—Leave Providence at 7 20 & 11 45 A. M. and 4 20 & 7 00 P. M. Distance 43 miles.

RALEIGH & GASTON RAILWAY.

Leave Raleigh for Gaston, Weldon, and way stations, at 8 15 A. M.
Returning—Leave Weldon at 11 00 A. M. Distance 97 miles.

RARITAN & DELAWARE BAY RAILWAY.

Leave New York for Port Monmouth, Manchester, Camden, and way stations, at **11 00** A. M. and 4 00, 5 00 & **5 00** P. M.
Returning—Leave Camden at **3 30** & **9 20** A. M. and **2 30** P. M. Distance 112 miles.

READING & COLUMBIA RAILWAY.

Leave Reading for Columbia, and way stations, at 6 10 A. M. and 6 15 P. M.
Returning—Leave Columbia at 7 30 A. M. and 2 45 P. M. Distance 46 miles.

RICHMOND & DANVILLE RAILWAY.

Leave Richmond for Burkeville, Danville, and way stations, at 8 00 & 9 45 A. M.
Returning—Leave Danville at 5 45 A. M. Distance 141 miles.

RICHMOND & PETERSBURG RAILWAY.

Leave Richmond for Petersburg, and way stations, at 4 20 A. M. and 4 40 P. M.
Returning—Leave Pocahontas at 6 25 A. M. and 5 30 P. M. Distance 21 miles.

RICHMOND, FREDERICKSBURG & POTOMAC RAILWAY.

Leave Washington for Fredericksburg, Richmond, and way stations at 6 45 A. M. and 7 00 P. M.
Returning—Leave Richmond at 8 15 A. M. and 8 00 P. M. Distance 130 miles.

ROME, WATERTOWN & OGDENSBURG RAILWAY.

Leave Rome for Watertown, Ogdensburg, Potsdam Junction, and way stations, at 5 10 A. M., and 12 15 & 5 10 P. M.
Returning—Leave Potsdam Junction at 7 10 A. M. and 1 40 & 8 00 P. M. Distance 148 miles.

RUTLAND & BURLINGTON RAILWAY.

Leave Bellows Falls for Rutland, Brandon, Burlington, and way stations, at 11 40 A. M. and 5 45 & 10 05 P. M.
Returning—Leave Burlington at 10 00 A. M., and 2 45, 5 00 & 10 00 P. M. Distance 120 miles.

ST. LOUIS & IRON MOUNTAIN RAILWAY.

Leave St. Louis for Potosi, Pilot Knob, and way stations, at 6 15 A. M., and for De Soto at 6 15 A. M. and 4 00 P. M.
Returning—Leave Pilot Knob at 3 00 P. M., and De Soto at 6 00 A. M. and 5 35 P. M. Distance 87 miles.

SANDUSKY, DAYTON & CINCINNATI RAILWAY.

Leave Sandusky for Bellefontaine, Springfield, Cincinnati, and way stations, at 10 00 A. M. and 7 35 P. M.
Returning—Leave Cincinnati at 7 00 A. M. and 6 00 P. M. Distance 215 miles.

SANDUSKY, MANSFIELD & NEWARK RAILWAY.

Leave Sandusky for Newark, and way stations, at 7 20 A. M. and 6 15 P. M.
Returning—Leave Newark at 6 00 A. M. and 12 30 P. M Distance 116 miles.

SCHUYLKILL & SUSQUEHANNA RAILWAY.

Leave Harrisburg for Auburn, and way stations, at 3 20 P. M.
Returning—Leave Auburn at 7 50 A. M. and 1 50 P. M. Distance 59 miles.

SHORE LINE (CONN.) RAILWAY.

Leave New Haven for New London, at 7 00 & 10 55 A. M., and **3 15**, 6 05 & **11 15** P. M.
Returning—Leave New London at **12 10**, 6 40 & 11 10 A. M., and **2 35** & 5 15 P. M. Distance 50 miles.

SOUTH CAROLINA RAILWAY.

Leave Charleston for Branchville, Columbia, Augusta, and way stations, at 7 00 A. M.
Returning—Leave Augusta at 7 10 A. M.; Columbia at 6 00 A. M. Distance 137 miles.

SOUTH WESTERN & MUSCOGEE RAILWAY.

Leave Macon for Fort Valley, Columbus, and way stations, at 7 23 A. M.; for Eufalia, 7 23 A. M.
Returning—Leave Columbus at 7 00 A. M.; Eufalia at 5 10 A. M. Distance 99 miles.

STONINGTON & PROVIDENCE RAILWAY.

Leave Providence for Stonington, New London, and way stations, at 7 10 A. M., and **12 35**, 1 00, 4 00, **7 12** & **10 00** P. M.
Returning—Leave New London at **1 40** and 6 15 A. M., and **5 15** P. M.

SYRACUSE & BINGHAMTON RAILWAY.

Leave Syracuse for Binghamton, and way stations, at 8 00 A. M. and 7 00 P. M.
Returning—Leave Binghamton at 7 00 A. M. and 4 10 P. M. Distance 80 miles.

SYRACUSE & OSWEGO RAILWAY.

Leave Oswego for Syracuse, and way stations, at 8 00 A. M. and 2 00 P. M.
Returning—Leave Syracuse at 7 10 A. M. and 2 30 P. M.

TERRE HAUTE & INDIANAPOLIS RAILWAY.

Leave Indianapolis for Terre Haute, St. Louis, and way stations, at 8 30 A. M., and 12 55, 3 10 & 10 15 P. M.
Returning—Leave St. Louis at 7 40 A. M. and 5 40 P. M. Distance 262 miles.

TOLEDO, WABASH & WESTERN RAILWAY.

Leave Toledo for Fort Wayne, Lafayette, Decatur, Quincy, and way stations, at 1 20 A. M. and 1 00 P. M.
Returning—Leave Quincy at 4 00 A. M. and 4 30 P. M. Distance 476 miles.

TOLEDO, LOGANSPORT & BURLINGTON RAILWAY.

Leave Logansport for State Line, Peoria, and way stations, at 9 40 A. M. and 9 00 P. M.
Returning—Leave Peoria at 10 00 A. M. and 9 20 P. M. Distance 172 miles.

TROY & BOSTON RAILWAY.

(See full Tables on page 79)

UNION PACIFIC RAILWAY.

Leave Wyandotte for Lawrence, Topeka, and way stations, at 7 00 A. M.
Returning—Leave Topeka at 1 30 P. M. Distance 70 miles.

UTICA & BLACK RIVER RAILWAY.

Leave Utica for Trenton Falls, Boonville, and way stations, at 11 25 A. M. and 5 00 P. M.
Returning—Leave Boonville at 7 10 A. M. and 2 05 P. M. Distance 35 miles.

VERMONT CENTRAL RAILWAY.

Leave Bellows' Falls for Montpelier, Burlington, St. Albans, Montreal, and way stations, at 11 45 A. M. and 10 00 P. M.
Returning—Leave Montreal at 8 30 A. M. and 3 30 P. M.

VERMONT & MASSACHUSETTS RAILWAY.

Leave Fitchburg for Athol, Greenfield, Brattleboro, and way stations, at 9 15 A. M. and 1 20 P. M.
Returning—Leave Brattleboro at 8 55 A. M., and Greenfield at 9 25 A. M. and 2 40 P. M. Distance 69 miles.

VIRGINIA CENTRAL RAILWAY.

Leave Richmond for Gordonsville, Staunton, Jackson's River, and way stations, at 7 15 A. M. and 7 15 P. M.
Returning—Leave Jackson's River at 1 30 P. M.; Staunton at 8 00 A. M. Distance 195 miles.

VIRGINIA & TENNESSEE RAILWAY.

Leave Lynchburg for Dublin, Bristol, and way stations, at 5 30 P. M.
Returning—Leave Bristol at 4 25 P. M. Distance 204 miles.

WELLAND RAILWAY.

Leave Port Dalhousie for St. Catharines, Port Colborne, and way stations, at 7 30 A. M. and 2 15 P. M.
Returning—Leave Port Colborne at 10 45 A. M. and 5 00 P. M. Distance 25 miles.

WESTERN (MASS.) RAILWAY.

Leave Albany for Pittsfield, Springfield, Worcester, Boston, and way stations, at 6 30 & **9 50** A. M., and **4 45** & 9 10 P. M.
Returning—Leave Worcester at 6 15 & **10 05** A. M., and **4 00**, 4 15, **8 00** & **10 00** P. M.
Distance to Boston 200 miles.

WESTERN UNION RAILWAY.

Leave Racine for Elkhart, Beloit, Freeport, Savanna, Fulton and Port Byron, at 10 00 A. M. and 9 00 P. M.
Returning—Leave Port Byron at 7 30 A. M. and 6 50 P. M. Distance 181 miles.

WESTERN & ATLANTIC RAILWAY.

Leave Chattanooga for Dalton, Kingston, Atlanta, and way stations, at 5 50 A. M. and 6 10 P. M.
Returning—Leave Atlanta at 7 30 A. M. and 7 30 P. M.

WEST JERSEY, CAPE MAY & MILLVILLE RAILWAY.

Leave Philadelphia for Glassboro, Salem, Cape May, and way stations, at 8 00 & **9 00** A. M., and 3 00, 3 30 & 6 00 P. M.
Returning—Leave Cape May at 6 30 & 9 00 A. M.; Salem at 7 00 A. M. and 3 35 P. M.

WILMINGTON & MANCHESTER RAILWAY.

Leave Wilmington for Florence, Kingsville, and way stations, at 8 50 P. M.
Returning—Leave Kingsville at 3 00 P. M. Distance 171 miles.

WILMINGTON & WELDON RAILWAY.

Leave Wilmington for Goldsboro, Weldon, and way stations, at 3 30 A. M. and 1 00 P. M.
Returning—Leave Weldon at 11 00 A. M. and 9 00 P. M. Distance 162 miles.

WORCESTER & NASHUA RAILWAY.

Leave Worcester for Nashua, and way stations, at 6 30 & 11 15 A. M., and 4 20 P. M.
Returning—Leave Nashua at 7 10 A. M., 12 00 M., and 5 00 P. M. Distance 46 miles.

www.ingramcontent.com/pod-product-compliance
Lightning Source LLC
Chambersburg PA
CBHW020140170426
43199CB00010B/822
* 9 7 8 3 3 3 7 2 1 6 6 9 6 *